Stitch and Sew Home

Eline Pellinkhof

D&C
David and Charles

A DAVID & CHARLES BOOK

www.defonteintirion.nl
Originally published in the Netherlands as
Eline's Huis

First published in the UK and USA in 2012 by
F&W Media International, LTD

David & Charles is an imprint of
F&W Media International, LTD
Brunel House, Forde Close, Newton Abbot,
TQ12 4PU, UK

F&W Media International, LTD is a subsidiary of
F+W Media, Inc.
10151 Carver Road, Suite 200, Blue Ash,
OH 45242, USA

Front cover: Eline Pellinkhof
Photography: Joost de Wolf
Close-ups: Eline Pellinkhof
Back cover: Hans Guldemond
Design and Styling: Eline Pellinkhof
Layout: Antoinette van Schaik
Editing: Hanny Vlaar

A catalogue record for this book is available from the British Library.

ISBN-13: 978-1-4463-0235-4 paperback
ISBN-10: 1-4463-0235-0 paperback

Printed in China.

10 9 8 7 6 5 4 3 2 1

Contents:

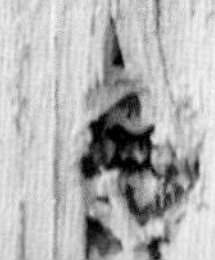

Welcome to Eline's House!

My house is not big, but it is cosy and bright. I like to decorate with a combination of styles and colours. I simply can't choose and there are so many things that I like. I love, for instance, cross stitch samplers, vintage postcards featuring old postage stamps and handwritten script, crocheted lace and brightly coloured fabrics from far off lands, cards and lettering, flowers from the garden, cut out silhouettes ... my home has all.

Why go shopping for unqiue and contemporary home decorations when you can make them yourself, easily, at low cost and exactly as you want them? This book is packed full of designs for you to copy by following the patterns and clear instructions. I have designed the cheerful fabric and many of the craft materials myself especially for this book. Joost de Wolf's wonderful photographs complete the picture, providing inspiration for anyone who, like me, is a fan of contemporary and vintage designs, of roses and embroidery, fabric and paper. In short, welcome to my house!

Eline

A brief introduction

Welcome to my house. I am Eline Pellinkhof. After attending fashion school and many years of working as a freelance children's clothes designer, I stumbled into the world of crafts. I now design clipart, stamps and patterned paper, mainly for my favourite producer and client Marianne Design, which others then use to make pretty things. I wanted to see if I could create my own project ideas with all the materials I have designed. And I found that I could! What's more, they became a book. A book of which I am extremely proud. But naturally I didn't do it all on my own, I received some 'home visits'. A number of creative ladies have helped me to produce this book. Each and every one is a star in their own right, and I am full of admiration for them all.

First there is Antoinette van Schaik, whom I have worked with for many years. We work together on the magazine *Marianne* and Antoinette always makes sure that my designs are 'ready to print'. Antoinette is also responsible for the layout of this book, and she produced various bags, pouches and other fabric items, as well as crocheting fabulous butterflies. (www.avormgevingendtp.nl and http://antoinettevanschaik.blogspot.com)

I have also worked with Hanny Vlaar many times in the past. I am very grateful to her for editing this book, which involved reading the texts repeatedly and making improvements.

Frences Lich has also been of huge assistance to me with a number of paper projects. I have been a fan of Frences' style of scrapbooking and card-making for many years. Her bunting (Project 41) is a true gem, incorporating so many ideas and sources of inspiration. (http://scrappenenbeppen.blogspot.com/)

Then we have Gepke Sjaardema from the web store Your Zoap, who has also been a massive help to me, this time with the styling for the photography. We photographed all the items in this book at her stylish shed in Lelystad. Nothing was too much for Gepke; she let me shift and move everything around, and use anything that I wanted to. (www.yourzoap.nl and http://rosadotje.blogspot.com)

I came to know Petra Hoeksema via an international blog course we both followed. Petra is a crocheter at heart, although she also often works with fabric. She crocheted the prettiest borders for my towels. I have also used lots of ribbons that Petra sells from her web store. (http://bypetra.nl/blog and http://bypetra.nl)

And last but not least, Helga Teunissen, who I met again after 25 years. She has done a great deal of embroidery work for me, including Project 28, and in no time at all! Every evening I received a new photo by e-mail showing the progress made that day, which meant I was able to see my embroidered designs gradually take shape.
(Helga makes lots of cards for http://kaartenmakerij.blogspot.com)

Keep an eye on my blog for any updates, downloads and new ideas for Eline's House: http://elinepellinkhof.blogspot.com

Eline's House materials

A short note on the Eline's House fabric

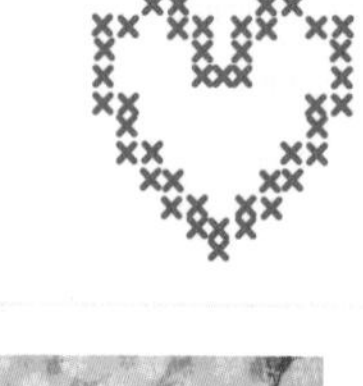

I have designed a patterned fabric especially for this book. However, as most craft shops don't have room for rolls of fabric in the store, we have decided to sell the fabric packaged by the metre. Each metre of fabric is 140cm wide and features nine different patterns and lots of borders, which complement each other perfectly. This means that you don't have to buy a load of separate pieces of fabric as you have everything you need in the one metre. To give you an even greater choice, this fabric is available in three colour combinations:

- Roses (neutral): pink, red and grey hues, item no. EL 8520
- Meadow (bright): pink, red, blue and grass-green hues, item no. EL 8521
- Vintage (pastel): pink, light blue and beige hues, item no. EL 8522

A fabric that goes very well with these patterns is Ikea's natural linen (Aina, natural colour), but of course they also look great when used together with other natural fabrics.

I have also put together a small collection of ribbons and lace: two white cotton lace trims, a white twilled ribbon featuring old-fashioned text, pink roses on a beige background, and a dark red ribbon with white polka dots and white picot border, item no. EL 8523.

Patterned paper.

Self-stamped twilled ribbon.

However, I have also used other beautiful ribbons in this book:
- All the narrow ribbons are from By Petra (http://bypetra.nl)
- All the wide ribbons (on pretty cardboard reels) are from the Ribbonstore (www.ribbonstore.nl)

Here is a great tip for stopping the synthetic trims from fraying: quickly run a flame along the ends - this melts the edges and stops it from fraying.

I had my heart set on using old-fashioned mother-of-pearl buttons in the collection just like those from grandma's button tins, and after a short search we found them! These beautiful buttons go perfectly with a wide range of styles and colours, item no. EL 8524.

I have also used self-cover buttons in various different sizes from Prym products, available through Coats Crafts (www.coatscrafts.co.uk and www.coatscrafts.com).

I have also used some pretty vintage stamps:
- with butterflies, item no. EC 0119
- with postmarks, item no. EC 0120
- with cross stitch patterns, item no. EC 0121

And then there are the two A4-sized blocks of natural patterned paper:
- Meadow, with lots of blue and green hues, butterflies and birds, item no. PB 7028
- Roses, with lots of pink, red and beige hues, roses and embroidery, item no. PB 7029

Note on crochet terms for US crafters
Some terms are different for the US from those used in the UK/Europe: in addition, the same term can be used to refer to different stitches as can be seen below. UK/Europe terms have been used for the patterns in this book:

UK/Europe	US
double crochet	single crochet
half treble crochet	half-double crochet
treble crochet	double crochet
double treble crochet	treble crochet

Grandma's button tins.

My grandfather collected plants and insects, and as a child I often went with him into the countryside, each of us carrying a large butterfly net to catch beetles with. My grandfather's study was full of cabinets, and these cabinets were full of drawers filled with pinned insects. I loved to spend hours looking at them and this, I think, is the reason why I have never been afraid of 'creepy crawlies'. I'm sad to say that the entire collection went to a museum and I don't have even a small drawer of beetles to hang on the wall. So I decided to make one myself...

PROJECT 1

Display boxes

Split-wood butterfly boxes

Cut out a background of patterned paper to line the inside of the boxes. Print butterfly stamps onto patterned paper and cut them out. Stick together two bodies to make each butterfly, preferably one small butterfly on top of a larger butterfly in the same shape. Attach the bodies securely to the background paper and machine stitch across the body. Fold the wings upwards slightly. Pierce around the postage stamps on the printed paper with the hole punch and tear out. Stick the postage stamps to the background paper using foam tape and further decorate the background with label stamps. Stick two or three square pieces of foam board on top of each other inside the boxes. (They don't need to be perfectly cut to fit as they won't be visible.) Finally, stick the decorated backgrounds onto the foam board inside the boxes, and stick pins through the bodies of the butterflies.

What you'll need:
Eline's House stamps and patterned paper,
buttons,
split-wood boxes,
foam board,
pins,
foam tape,
very fine hole punch,
sewing machine

Wooden butterfly box

Cut out a piece of foam board a little smaller than the internal dimensions of the box frame. Cover the foam board with linen using strips of double-sided adhesive plastic to stick the fabric to the back of the board. Use glue or double-sided tape to stick a ribbon and a lace border to the top and bottom edges of the foam board, and decorate with punched out postage stamps, labels and buttons.

Print various butterfly stamps onto the linen fabric and roughly cut around them. Use same size pieces of double-sided adhesive plastic to stick the linen fabric to the patterned fabric and carefully cut out the butterflies. (The stamps now appear on the linen underside of the butterflies and are actually only used so that you can cut around them.) Fold the butterflies double and machine stitch from the head straight along the fold, around 5 mm to 1 cm (¼ to ⅜ in) down. This enables you to raise the wings slightly.

First stick two layers of foam board into the box (this can be very rough, as it won't be visible) and stick the covered piece of foam board on top. Push pins through the butterflies and stick them into the foam board.

What you'll need:
'Vintage' patterned fabric,
Eline's House stamps,
Eline's House ribbon and buttons,
linen fabric,
wooden box frame,
double-sided adhesive plastic,
foam board,
pins,
foam tape,
very fine hole punch,
sewing machine

PROJECT 2

Butterfly clothes pegs

Cut various butterflies out of butterfly patterned paper; alternatively, print butterfly stamps onto patterned paper. Cut strips of patterned paper to the size of the clothes peg. Stick only the bodies of the butterflies to the strips and machine stitch together. Fold the wings upwards slightly. Stick the butterfly strips onto the clothes pegs.

Thread the decorated clothes pegs onto a string and stretch the string above your workbench. Use to hang up cards, photos, notices and other bits and bobs.

What you'll need:
clothes pegs,
patterned paper,
butterfly stamps,
sewing machine

Roses
are red
Violets
are blue
Sugar
is sweet
And so
are
you
594
6'''
8'''

My great-grandmother had a wonderful album with loose sheets, on which friends could write a message, an 'Album Amicorum', a precursor of the traditional Dutch 'album of verses'. Some of the pages in this album were embroidered with pretty old-fashioned roses and the paper or cardboard was perforated all over with tiny holes. Stitching paper similar to this is still available today, and I have used it to embroider a pretty little rose design, just like those in my great-grandmother's album.

What's great about stitching paper is that not only is it easy to embroider, but you can also cut out attractive lacy edges and shapes. This takes a lot of precision because you always need to cut from hole to hole, but you can produce excellent results. First use a fine pencil to draw the cutting lines onto the back of the paper, and then use a very sharp knife to cut the design out.

PROJECT 3

Stitching paper rose

Rose print

Embroider the rose cross stitch chart D (see Patterns) onto a piece of white stitching paper. Cut the stitching paper so that it is 46 holes* wide and 64 holes high, and cut out a piece of ecru stitching paper 68 holes wide and 86 holes high.

Use a pencil to trace the border/corner pattern on the back of the ecru paper and carefully cut out the crosses. Always cut from hole to hole.

Stick the white stitching paper together with a piece of ribbon in the centre of the ecru stitching paper and backstitch around the outer edge. Sew on a button.

* NOTE: Cut through hole 1 and through hole 46, and you will therefore be left with 44 full holes.

What you'll need:
white and ecru stitching paper,
DMC thread,
ribbon and button,
sharp knife

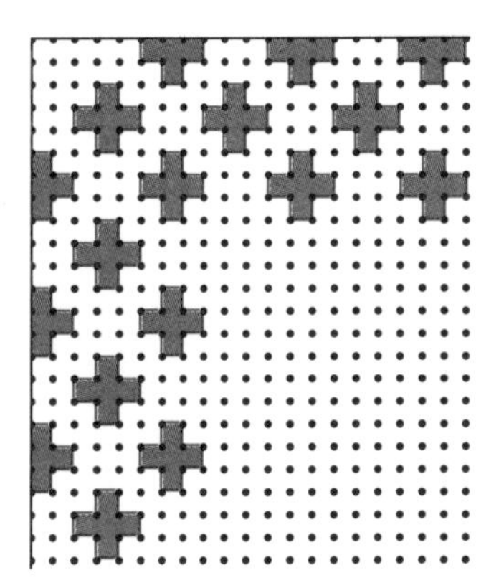

Border/corner pattern.

Roses are red, Violets are blue.
ABCDE
FGHIJ
KLMN
O
P
QRSTU
VWXY
WXYZ
Z
Home Sweet Home
Roses are red,
Violets are blue,
Sugar is sweet,

PROJECT 6

Stamped photo frame

Print with the stamps onto the picture mount, concentrating on two opposite corners. Print label and flower stamps onto patterned paper and cut them out. Place linen and ribbon behind the mount and print a heart stamp in the upper left panel. Distress the edges of the photo and the frame slightly. Stick down the photo and the decorative elements to make an attractive collage. Finish by stamping a text onto the frame itself.

What you'll need:
white photo frame 21.5 x 21.5 cm (8¾ x 8¾ in) with a four-square aperture mount,
linen fabric,
Eline's House stamps and patterned paper,
ribbon (Ribbonstore),
strip of lace,
button,
black and red inkpads,
photograph

This frame came with a mount, but you can also cut one out yourself: cut four 5 cm (2 in) squares from thick cardboard.

Printing stamps

but not on paper

For a while now I've been exploring what else can be done with flexible, clear stamps apart from just printing ink on paper. I've already tried out a few ideas. Printing stamps onto fabric, for instance, which works very well and gives great results. Printing stamps onto white or light-coloured cotton twilled ribbon also looks great, and allows you to design your own trims.

As the clear stamps are flexible, you can also use them to print stamps onto non-flat surfaces such as pebble stones. Instead of attaching the stamp to a Perspex block, carefully press it onto the stone with your hand. You can create a lovely decorative display simply grouping together a number of pretty stamped stones.

Roses are red,
Violets are blue,
Sugar is sweet,
and so are you.

Clay pendants

I then went on to test whether I could also print stamps into clay. The stamps are raised, and these raised sections look great when printed into a simple piece of white clay. I purchased some self-hardening white clay and used a plastic bottle to roll it flat. I bought some mini cake moulds – a heart, a flower and a butterfly – and I cut out the other shapes myself. A small ball of clay, flattened slightly, with a postmark stamped into it looks just like a wax seal.

Use a skewer to prick holes in the stamped shapes so that you can suspend them or sew them onto fabric or paper. I have used these clay shapes to great effect in many of the designs in this book: on cushions, on cards, as pendants and as decorative beads on a string. .

Embroidering clay

I decided to make more holes in the clay. Not so that I could suspend the shapes, but so that I could embroider them with coloured thread once they were dry. Cross stitch, a blanket stitch border, backstitch and even chain stitch worked well (see Embroidery stitches).

NOTE: You can also try pressing other textures into the clay, for example small crocheted flowers, lace or coarse linen.

Clay beads

Use both hands to roll a clay sphere, and push a cocktail stitck (toothpick) through the middle. Then press two small flower stamps onto both sides of the sphere at the same time. Remove the stamps, carefully slide out the cocktail stick (toothpick) and leave the bead to dry.

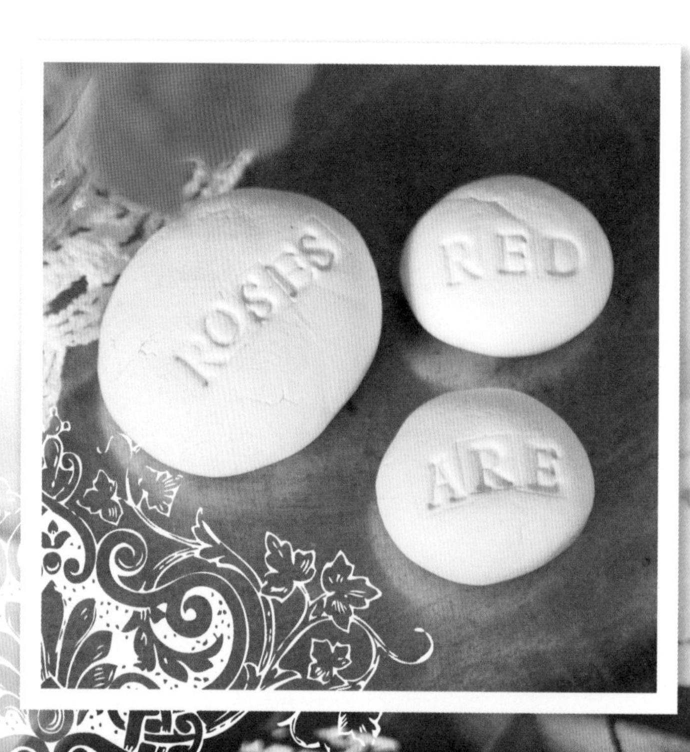

Clay stones with lettering

First model a few 'pebble stones' and then push letter stamps into them to make words.

Colouring clay

The clay can easily be coloured using Copic markers once dry. Paint will also work well.

Crocheted clay

I asked Petra to try crocheting borders around clay discs which proved very successful. A large clay was flattened into a disc by rolling with a small bottle, and decorated by printing with a stamp. A border of holes were then pierced around the edge, about 5 mm to 1 cm (¼ to ⅜ in) apart. Petra first worked a blanket stitch around the edge, and to this she then stitched the border from the guest towel (see Project 8).

PROJECT 7

Cards

Roses are red, Violets are blue,
Sugar is sweet, and so are you.

Home sweet home

Decorate the card with pieces of fabric and paper, and stick lace paper on top. Tie string around the card and tie on a ribbon. The rosettes are made from two paper circles measuring 4 cm (1½ in) and 5 cm (2 in) in diameter. Draw a spiral on each circle from the centre outwards, and cut from the outside inwards along the spiral. Roll the outer point towards the centre. When you have almost reached the end, apply a little textile adhesive to the flap at the back and fix down the rolled up paper. Pierce the rose embroidery pattern A (see Patterns) and embroider with DMC threads. Stick the paper rosettes to the card.

What you'll need:
white single fold card
13.5 x 13.5 cm (5¼ x 5¼ in),
'Vintage' patterned fabric,
Eline's House patterned paper,
lace paper,
string,
ribbon,
DMC threads,
paper piercer

Clay bird box

Cut a piece of paper measuring 13 x 13 cm (5 x 5 in) and distress the edges. Cut a piece of fabric measuring 11.5 x 11.5 cm (4½ x 4½ in). Layer the fabric on top of the paper and machine stitch to the card. Cut a large decorative motif from patterned paper, decorate further with stamped images and layer on top of a lace paper circle; stick this to the card. Stick on a scrunched up lace-embellished fabric strip and sew on the stamped clay shape using DMC thread.

What you'll need:
white single fold card
13.5 x 13.5 cm (5¼ x 5¼ in),
Eline's House patterned paper
and stamps,
'Vintage' patterned fabric,
Eline's House ribbon,
lace paper,
clay shape (see Project 6, Clay pendants),
sewing machine

Love you xxx

Cut two strips of patterned paper measuring 6.5 x 12.5 cm and 5 x 12.5 cm (2½ x 4⅞ in and 2 x 4⅞ in), print with stamps and join together with adhesive tape. Run the serrated knife along the edges to distress, and hide the join with a folded strip of lace and ribbon. Wrap the string around the bottom of the paper and tie in a bow. Stick the paper square to the card. Cut small leaves out of linen. Print label stamps onto patterned paper and cut out. Make two paper rosettes (see Home sweet home card). To make a fabric rosette: stick down a thin strip of fabric in the centre of a paper circle, and turn the fabric; apply a thin layer of textile adhesive to the paper, and continue to turn the fabric to stick it onto the paper. Fix the leaves, labels and rosettes to the card.

What you'll need:
white single fold card
13.5 x 13.5 cm (5¼ x 5¼ in),
Eline's House patterned paper
and stamps,
red inkpad,
linen fabric and 'Vintage'
patterned fabric,
ribbon (Ribbonstore),
lace and string,
serrated knife

Embroidered rose

Cut two strips of patterned paper 4 x 13.5 cm (1½ x 5¼ in) and punch a border along the long edges. Cut a strip 5.5 x 13.5 cm (2¼ x 5¼ in) from a different patterned paper, and print a text onto this using stamps. Stick the paper strips to the card; fold lace and ribbon around the card front to hide the joins. Print leaf stamps onto green paper and cut out leaving an outline. Embroider the rose cross stitch chart F (see Patterns) and a running stitch border onto a piece of stitching paper measuring 5.5 x 4.5 cm (2¼ x 1¾ in and stick this between the leaves. Print small flower stamps onto patterned paper and stick onto the card.

What you'll need:
white single fold card
13.5 x 13.5 cm (5¼ x 5¼ in),
Eline's House patterned paper
and stamps,
black inkpad,
white stitching paper,
lace,
red ribbon,
border punch

Wax seal with butterflies

Print stamps onto a piece of fabric measuring 13 x 13 cm (5 x 5 in), and machine stitch to the front of the card along the sides and lower edge. Pad the fabric with a small amount of fibrefill and stitch down the top edge. Cut notches in five places and insert the brads. Print a label stamp onto patterned paper and cut it out. Print two butterfly stamps onto white paper, colour them in a bit and cut them out. Stick the stamped images onto the card along with a ribbon, and stitch the wax seal clay shape onto the ribbon.

What you'll need:
white single fold card
13.5 x 13.5 cm ($5\frac{1}{4}$ x $5\frac{1}{4}$ in),
Eline's House patterned paper
and stamps,
red and black inkpads,
'Vintage' patterned fabric,
ribbon (Ribbonstore),
wax seal clay shape
(see Project 6, Clay pendants),
5 white brads,
fibrefill,
sewing machine

Postcard

Tear out a piece of patterned fabric measuring 12.5 x 12.5 cm ($4\frac{7}{8}$ x $4\frac{7}{8}$ in) and stick this to the card with textile glue. Print a postcard shape onto the linen using the postcard stamps. Punch out a postage stamp and print a stamp on top of this. Print a label stamp onto patterned paper and cut it out. Twist up a strip of white fabric (using patterned fabric) to make flowers (see Love you xxx card). Stick everything onto the card and tie a string with the label attached to it around the card.

What you'll need:
white single fold card
13.5 x 13.5 cm ($5\frac{1}{4}$ x $5\frac{1}{4}$ in),
Eline's House patterned paper
and stamps,
black ink,
'Vintage' patterned fabric,
linen fabric,
ribbon (Ribbonstore)

PROJECT 8

Crocheted borders

Towel

Mark each centimetre (3/8 in) just above the edge of the finish of the towel. Use the marks to create a blanket stitch the same size using crochet thread in the same colour as the towel, measuring 1 cm (3/8 in) in width and the same depth as the edge of the towel. Take 250 cm (100 in) of thread, fold double and tie a small knot at the end. Start by pulling the thread through a corner via the inside, and fasten by tying a small knot at the end on the inside.

Use thread in the same colour as the towel and start the crocheted border with 3 double crochets in each blanket stitch. This is the first row:
1st row: a base of double crochets in a multiple of 3
2nd row: 1 reverse chain, 1 double crochet in the 1st double crochet stitch, 5 chains, miss 2 double crochets, *1 double crochet in the next double crochet, 5 chains, miss 2 double crochets, repeat from* to the end of the towel
3rd row: *start with 2 slip stitches in the 1st arc of the 5 chains, 1 double crochet in the arc of the 5 chains, 11 chains, 1 treble crochet in the 5th chain from the needle, 1 treble crochet in the next chain and 1 half treble crochet in the next chain, slip stitch in the next chain, 7 chains, 1 treble crochet in the 5th chain from the needle, 1 treble crochet in the next chain and 1 half treble crochet in the next chain, slip stitch in the next chain, 2 chains, and a double crochet in the next arc of 5 chains from the previous row. 5 chains and 1 double crochet in the next arc of 5 chains from the previous row. 10 chains, 1 slip stitch in the 10th chain from the needle, 7 chains and 1 slip stitch in the 1st chain, 7 chains and 1 slip stitch in the 1st chain, 2 chains and 1 double crochet in the next arc of 5 chains from the previous row. 5 chains and 1 double crochet in the next arc of 5 chains from the previous row. Start again at *
4th row: stitch a new colour in each central petal of the petals made of chains. Crochet 5 chains and 1 slip stitch in the ring of chains that form the central petal, repeat this another 2 times, making three coloured petals in total.

What you'll need:
white towel 50 x 100 cm (20 x 40 in),
DMC Petra crochet cotton perle no. 5 in the same colour as the towel and three contrasting colours for the flower petals,
crochet hook 2 mm,
darning needle with a sharp point,
marker pen

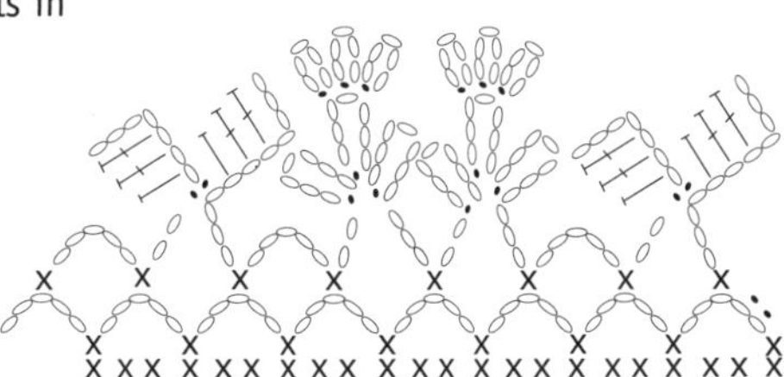

Guest towel

Cut four strips of fabric measuring 30 x 10 cm (12 x 4 in) and add in seam allowances. Place two strips with the right sides facing each other and stitch one long edge together. Press the seam open. Lay the strips open on the edge of the guest towel with the right sides facing. Stitch one strip to the guest towel. Fold the two strips back together with the right sides facing and stitch the two sides together. Fold and press the seam of the loose strip inwards (this will be stitched in place later). Repeat on the other side of the guest towel.

Mark each centimetre (3/8 in) on the underside of the fabric strips. Use the marks to sew a blanket stitch the same size using the crochet thread, measuring 1 cm (3/8 in) in width and 5 mm (1/4 in) in depth. Take 90 cm (1 yd) of thread and tie a small knot at the end. Start by pulling the thread through a corner via the inside, and fasten by tying a small knot at the end on the inside.

Start the crocheted border with 3 double crochets in each blanket stitch. This is the first row:
1st row: a base of double crochets in a multiple of 3
2nd row: 1 reverse chain, 4 chains, miss 2 double crochets and 1 double crochet in the 3rd double crochet. * 4 chains, miss 2 double crochets and 1 double crochet in the 3rd double crochet. Repeat from *
3rd row: 1 reverse chain, *3 double crochets in the loop of 4 chains from the previous row, 3 chains, 1 slip stitch in the last chained, 2 double crochets in the loop of 4 chains from the previous row. Repeat for each loop from *

Finally, stitch the still open seam of the two strips to the guest towel.

What you'll need:
white guest towel 30 x 50 cm (12 x 20 in),
'Meadow' patterned fabric,
DMC Petra crochet cotton perle no. 5,
crochet hook 2 mm,
darning needle with a sharp point,
marker pen

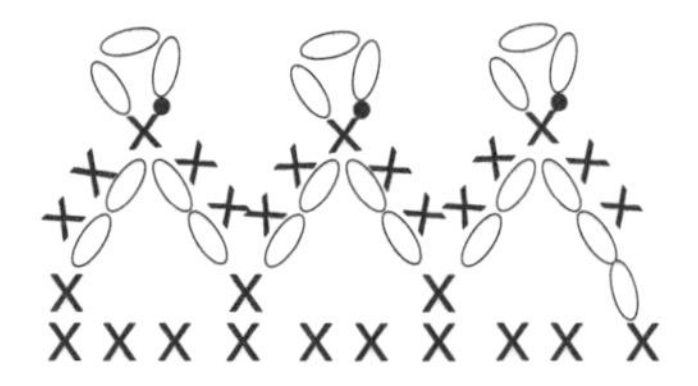

PROJECT 9

Gepke's soap chains

Grate the soap with a coarse grater. Add a little water so you get a dough-like lump. Roll it out until it is about 1 cm (3/8 in) thick and cut out shapes using metal cookie cutters, such as butterflies and hearts. Prick a hole in the soap shapes with a skewer. Now string together the soap shapes using white cord, threading on the beads, buttons and crocheted flowers and butterflies. Attach to the metal keychain. Attach lengths of ribbon to the keychain to finish.

Gepke made these pretty soap chains. Gepke holds workshops on how to make these chains at her wonderful shed/store/workshop space in Lelystad. Visit www.yourzoap.nl for more information.

What you'll need:
soap (not glycerin based),
metal cookie cutters,
Eline's House Ribbon,
buttons,
beads,
metal keychains,
white cord,
crocheted flower and butterfly

ROSES

PROJECT 10

Embroidered towel border

Embroider the border cross stitch chart J (see Patterns) onto the Aida trim. Pin this to the towel. Fold the ends of the ribbons around the embroidered trim and pin in place. Fold hems at the ends of the embroidered trim and pin them to the back of the towel. Stitch the embroidered trim in place.

What you'll need:
white towel 50 x 100 cm (20 x 40 in),
5 cm (2 in) wide Aida trim 55 cm (22in) long,
DMC threads,
ribbons

Frences makes this fantastic canvas with nine 'postage stamps' and an embroidered rose.

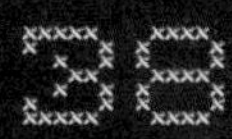

PROJECT 11

Canvas

Stick the lace paper to the canvas. Print stamps onto the canvas/lace paper. Cut seven pieces of patterned paper and one piece of linen measuring 3.5 x 4.5 cm ($1\frac{3}{8}$ x $1\frac{3}{4}$ in) and decorate all but one piece with stamps, ribbons, buttons and lace. Embroider the small rose cross stitch chart F (see Patterns) onto the stitching paper and stick it to the remaining piece of paper. Pierce the pattern for the large rose embroidery pattern B (see Patterns) into the canvas and embroider DMC threads. Stick the eight decorated pieces and the clay shape onto pieces of foam board measuring 3 x 4 cm ($1\frac{1}{8}$ x $1\frac{1}{2}$ in) and stick these onto the canvas.

What you'll need:

canvas 30 x 30 cm (12 x 12 in) and 4 cm ($1\frac{1}{2}$ in) thick,
lace paper in various sizes,
Eline's House patterned paper and stamps,
DMC threads,
foam board,
ribbon, buttons and lace,
clay shape 3.5 x 4.5 cm ($1\frac{3}{8}$ x $1\frac{3}{4}$ in) (see Project 6, Clay pendants),
piece of stitching paper 3 x 4 cm ($1\frac{1}{8}$ x $1\frac{1}{2}$ in)

No. 249
Roses are red, Violets are blue,
Sugar is sweet, and so are you.

PROJECT 12

Three mini canvases

Canvas 1: Butterfly

Make a double layer of fabric with double-sided adhesive plastic and thin wire in between, i.e. layer of fabric, layer of double-sided adhesive plastic, piece of very thin wire and finally another piece of fabric. Using a butterfly stamp as a template (stamp on the underside of the fabric), cut out two butterflies from the fabric sandwich. Print label and postmark stamps onto a piece of linen, and stick the linen, ribbon and lace paper to the canvas. Secure the butterflies to the canvas with a button and thread, and stitch on the clay shape.

Canvas 2: Fabric flower

Make a flower (see Project 30). Use a double layer of linen for the large flower and print a stamp on the top. Use a double layer of patterned fabric for the small flower. Stitch a small button onto a piece of linen measuring 4 x 4 cm ($1\frac{1}{2}$ x $1\frac{1}{2}$ in) and use this to cover the self-cover button (see Project 15). Cut out two linen circles with a diameter of 6 cm ($2\frac{3}{8}$ in) and fray around the edges. Join together in two cone shapes. Tie a thread with a needle to the button and stitch through the two circles, then through the smallest flower and then through the large flower. Fasten to the largest flower, but leave the thread in place. Stick a square piece of double-sided adhesive plastic in the centre of the canvas and cut a cross into this (through the canvas) measuring 3 x 3 cm ($1\frac{1}{8}$ x $1\frac{1}{8}$ in). Position the flower on the canvas, push the threaded needle through the cross, then carefully press the flower a little way into the cross and stick down.

Canvas 3: Crochet flower

Make a linen leaf (see Project 300, position the wire on one side and bend into a curve. Print a text onto patterned fabric using stamps and stick it to the along with lace paper beneath. Stick the leaf down and then fasten two crocheted flowers on top with a small button. Make a bow from coarse string and sew this to the canvas. Thread a clay bead (see Project 6) onto the end and stick this bead to the canvas.

What you'll need:
Three canvases 10 x 10 cm (4 x 4 in),
'Vintage' patterned fabric,
linen fabric,
string,
Eline's House ribbon and buttons,
Eline's House stamps,
double-sided adhesive plastic,
lace paper,
clay shapes (see Project 6, Clay pendants),
thin wire,
crocheted flowers,
19 mm self-cover button

The marker roll has been designed for neatly storing Copic markers all together, but can of course also be used for coloured pencils or paint brushes. The size of the roll and the storage compartments can be adjusted accordingly.

PROJECT 13

Marker roll

From the 'Roses' patterned fabric cut out the grey-with-lace pattern section rectangle A measuring 52 x 24 cm (20¾ x 9½ in) for the outside of the marker roll, a rectangle B measuring 52 x 24 cm (20¾ x 9½ in) for the inside of the marker roll, and a rectangle C measuring 52 x 15 cm (20¾ x 5⅝ in) for the storage compartments. (These measurements include a seam allowance.) Reinforce rectangles B and C using interfacing. Hem the top edge of rectangle C and stitch a strip of lace along the length. Place B and C on top of each other, aligning the bottom edges, and stitch together – this is easier to do once you have stitched the compartments for storing the markers. You will need to sew the first line of stitches 3 cm (1⅛ in) from the left edge, with the following lines 2.5 cm (1 in) apart. Faintly mark out the stitching lines using a pencil or chalk marker before sewing with a backstitch.

For the roll fastening, cut two pieces of the 'Roses are red' trim measuring 75 cm (29½ in) and 22 cm (8⅝ in). Pin the long trim in the centre of rectangle A (it should stick out to the right of the rectangle). Sew down the long trim approx. 1 cm (⅜ in) from the right edge. Sew down the smaller piece of trim 26 cm (10⅛ in) from the left edge of rectangle A. Pin the fabric pieces together with right sides facing, making sure that the ribbon will not be stitched into the seam! Stitch the seam together 1 cm (⅜ in) from the edge and leave a 12 cm (4¾ in) gap for turning. Turn the marker roll inside out, hem up the seam and topstitch around the edge. Decorate the roll with small buttons and a crocheted butterfly.

What you'll need:
'Roses' patterned fabric,
interfacing,
Eline's House "Roses are red'
trim, lace, and buttons,
crocheted butterfly (see
Project 46),
DMC thread,
sewing machine

Roses are red,
Violets are blue,
Sugar is sweet,
and so are you.
Roses are red,
Violets are blue,
Sugar is sweet,
and so are you.
Roses are red,
Violets are blue,
Sugar is sweet,
and so are you.

No. 280 Butterfly Specimen

A display of all sorts of labels, buttons, trims and crocheted decorations, clay shapes and pebble stones, neatly arranged.

PROJECT 14

Shadow box

Decorate the labels (see below for some special tips). Arrange the labels and all the items in the wooden box frame until you are happy with them. Then attach the buttons to the labels with thread and stick everything securely into the box frame with double-sided adhesive plastic. Use foam tape to fix the clay shapes and stones in place.

For the crochet flower label Use a pencil to sketch a pretty scroll shape. Pierce a hole every 5 mm (1/4 in) and embroider with black thread.

For the linen-covered label Use lace paper as a template to stipple on white textile paint for lovely results!

What you'll need:

- wooden box frame,
- paper labels,
- clay shapes (see Project 6),
- lace paper,
- stamped stones (see Project 6),
- crocheted flowers,
- Eline's House ribbon,
- buttons and patterned paper,
- string,
- very fine hole punch,
- black thread,
- linen fabric,
- white textile paint

VICTORIA STATION

PROJECT 15

Fabric-covered buttons

I have used self-covered buttons often in this book. I've covered these buttons with patterned fabric, with embroidered patches, with ribbon and even lace. It may be painstaking work, but with patience, skill and a small pair of pointed scissors you can produce great results.

Cut out discs of fabric to the desired size (see the back of the button packet for a working drawing). Use a small piece of double-sided tape to stick the button to the centre of the fabric. One by one, push small pieces of fabric tight over the 'teeth' using the point of the scissors. Go round and round until all the fabric is tightly secured and there are no more creases around the edge of the button. Finally, place the seal on the back of the button so that the letters are legible and press firmly until you hear it click.

NOTE: I used four sizes – 29 mm, 23 mm, 19 mm and 15 mm.

What you'll need:
self-cover buttons,
fabric,
double-sided tape,
pointed scissors

PROJECT 16

Bookmark

Embroider the border cross stitch chart G (see Patterns) onto a piece of stitching paper. Cut it out so that it is 25 holes in width and 91 holes in length. Take a piece of stitching paper measuring 5 x 15 cm (2 x 5⁶/₈ in) and trace the border/corner pattern (see Project 3) on the back along one long and one short edge. Cut it out, always cutting from hole to hole. Stick the embroidered part to the larger piece with the bottom edge and one side lined up exactly. Sew the border together with blanket stitch and the rest with backstitch.

What you'll need:
white stitching paper,
black DMC thread,
sharp knife

A few self-cover buttons on a label make a lovely gift.

PROJECT 17

Bracelet

Embroider the butterfly cross stitch chart B (see Patterns) and use it to cover a 29 mm self-cover button. Cover the other buttons with patterned fabric. Attach the buttons to the bracelet with small jump rings.

What you'll need:

- 'Meadow' patterned fabric,
- white 14-count Aida,
- DMC thread,
- self-cover buttons of various sizes,
- chain bracelet,
- small jump rings,
- small pair of pliers

Wooden embroidery hoops can make an excellent wall decoration. Here I used hoops of varying sizes: one 25 cm (10 in), two 20 cm (8 in), one 15 cm (5⅝ in) and one 10 cm (4 in). Combine matching patterned fabrics and embroidery work to make an attractive display.

PROJECT 18

Embroidery hoop pictures

Place a layer of white cotton under the patterned fabric so that the fabric does not show through. Open the hoop and place the smallest part under the double layer of fabric. Place the large circle at the top edge of the fabric on top of the small circle. Pull the fabric nice and tight and turn the screw at the top to safely secure. If you are using ribbon and/or lace, first stick this in place with a small amount of textile adhesive before you put the hoops in place. Cut the fabric short at the back.

Cover some buttons with patterned fabric or with an embroidered rose (see Project 15), and stitch to the fabric. Embroider a red zigzag stitch onto the ribbon and the lace. Embroider part of the printed cross stitch pattern for the large rose (I only embroidered the red, but you can embroider over the whole rose if you choose to). For rose cross stitch charts, see Patterns.

What you'll need:
Five wooden embroidery hoops of varying sizes,
'Roses' patterned fabric,
thin white cotton fabric,
white 14-count Aida,
DMC threads,
Eline's House ribbon,
self-cover buttons

POSTCARD
1922
vintage
3
2 cent
2 cent
2 cent
2 cent
Roses are red
Roses are red

PROJECT 19

Cushion covers

To make the cushion fronts
Cut out three lengths of linen measuring 40 x 40 cm (15⅝ x 15⅝ in) and add in seam allowances). Copy the stencils (see Patterns) and cut them out of plastic sheeting. Stipple the stencils with black textile paint onto the linen fabric and onto a piece of patterned fabric measuring 22 x 17 cm (8⅝ x 6¾ in) – choose a paint that gives good coverage.

Scan the postage stamp transfer (see Patterns) and print this out four times onto transfer paper. Iron the transfer images onto white cotton according to the manufacturer's instructions.

Fold and pin back the edges of the postage stamps (to make the stamps smaller fold back a wider border). Pin the postage stamps to the cushions on top of a white lace border and stitch down. Colour the wax seal clay shapes with red Copic ink and attach to the pieces of red ribbon; sew onto the cushion fronts.

To make the cushion backs
For each cushion, cut out two lengths from patterned fabric the same width as the front and half the height of the front plus 5 cm (2 in). So for a cushion cover measuring 40 x 40 cm (15⅝ x 15⅝ in), for example, cut out two lengths measuring 40 x 25 cm (15⅝ x 9⅞ in), remembering to add in seam allowances. Stitch a hem along one long edge of each length of fabric.

Position the cushion front with the right side facing upwards. Place one cushion back length on top with the right side facing down, lining up the bottom edge and the sides. Place the second length on top right side facing down, lining up the top edge and the sides. The two lengths should overlap by 10 cm (4 in) in the centre of the cushion. Pin and stitch all around the outer edge. Turn the cover inside out and press the seams open. You can leave the closing as it is, or add buttons and button holes, or attach ribbon ties. Insert the cushion pad to finish.

What you'll need:
linen fabric,
'Roses' patterned fabric,
white cotton fabric,
Eline's House lace trim,
plastic sheeting,
black textile paint,
stiff brush,
press-on transfer paper for printers,
red ribbon (Ribbonstore),
two wax seal clay shapes (see Project 6, Clay pendants),
cushion pad

ABCDE
FGHIJ
KLMNO
P
QRSTU
VWXY
Z

My mother always cleans the covers of library books she has borrowed before reading them, because she doesn't like the idea that they have already passed through lots of other hands. A nicer way to read a well-thumbed book without worrying about hygiene is to make a fabric book cover. This book cover has an adjustable flap on the back, so that it can be used with books of varying thicknesses.

PROJECT 20

Book cover

Embroider the ABC cross stitch chart I (see Patterns) onto the Aida fabric. Use some textile adhesive to stick the strips of lace, ribbons and pieces of linen on in the correct place. Embroider these on with different types of stitches and sew the buttons on top.

Refer to the book cover diagram (see Patterns). Mark out an area measuring 18.5 x 13 cm (7¼ x 5 in) around the embroidery. Stitch a piece of linen measuring 13 x 2 cm (5 x ¾ in) plus seam allowances to the top and lower edge of the embroidery and press the seams flat. Then stitch a piece of linen measuring 9 cm (3½ in) in width and 22.5 cm (8¾ in) in length to the right side of the embroidery and press the seam flat; make a hem at the edge of the linen strip. Stitch a piece of linen measuring 25 x 22.5 cm (9⅞ x 8¾ in) to the left edge of the embroidery and press the seam flat. Now fold back the right edge 8 cm (3⅛ in), over the embroidery. Take a piece of ribbon measuring around 25 cm (10 in) and position this upside down and vertically on the linen on the left edge, approximately 10 cm (4 in) from the embroidery, and pin down.

Cut out a piece of linen measuring 38 cm (15 in) in width and 22.5 cm (8¾ in) in height and place this on the front of the embroidery and the linen on the left edge. Stitch down the top, left edge and bottom edge, and stitch two corners as shown on the book cover diagram. Leave the right edge open and turn the cover inside out. Now slide the front of a book into the cover, and fold the flap back around it. Push the back of the book under the ribbon and fold the flap around the back of the book and therefore under the ribbon. For hard-cover books it may be better to use elastic here instead of ribbon.

What you'll need:
white 14-count Aida,
linen fabric,
Eline's House lace, ribbons and buttons,
ecru ribbons (Ribbonstore),
red and beige DMC thread

ROSES

PROJECT 21

Patchwork cushion

This cushion measures 37 x 50 cm (14½ x 20 in). Embroider the cross stitch border J (see Patterns) onto the Aida. Embroider all green sections beige and all light green sections light beige. Stitch a range of fabric strips and the embroidered strip together and press the seams flat. Stitch ribbons over the seams. Outline the measurements of the cushion on the back of the joined fabric and allow for seam allowances. Make an envelope back out of linen fabric (see Project 19).

What you'll need:
'Vintage' patterned fabric,
linen fabric,
white 14-count Aida,
DMC threads,
ribbons (Eline's House and By Petra)

HAKEN

Roses are red, Violets are blue

HAKEN

PROJECT 22

Petra's fabric baskets

Refer to the fabric baskets diagrams (see Patterns). Cut out 16 squares of patterned fabric measuring 7 x 7 cm (2¾ x 2¾ in) plus seam allowance, cut out a piece of linen measuring 28 x 21 cm (11 x 8¼ in) plus seam allowance and cut out a piece of red with white polka-dots fabric for the lining measuring 28 x 49 cm (11 x 19¼ in) plus seam allowance.

Set out eight squares (4 x 2). First stitch the horizontal lengths together. Press the seams flat. Then stitch the two rows together. Press the seams flat. Do the same again with the remaining eight squares. Stitch the two pieces of joined squares to the bottom and top edges of the linen. Press the seams flat and topstitch along the edge. Fold the linen in half, with the right sides facing. Stitch the side seams closed. Now open the pocket and rotate it a quarter turn. Close it again, but now with the two side seams together. There should be three triangles on the bottom edge. Mark a horizontal line where the triangle measures 14 cm (5½ in) in width (this is 7 cm/2¾ in from the tip) and stitch the triangles here. You have now created the base for the basket. Turn right side out.

Now take the lining fabric and fold in half with the right sides facing, then stitch up the side seams. To make the base, stitch the corners in the same way as for the outside of the basket. Slide the lining section into the outside section and pin both parts together in the corners and in the centre. Stitch the together in a straight line along the top edge. Pin the bias binding to the edge and stitch down from the inside (note, you will be able to see this on the outside). Fold back the top edge and press the basket into shape.

Petra also holds workshops on how to make these fabric baskets. Visit her website for information: http://bypetra.nl

What you'll need:
'Meadow' patterned fabric,
linen fabric,
red with white polka-dot fabric (By Petra),
60 cm (23½ in) bias binding (By Petra),
sewing machine

To make a label to identify the contents of the basket, print with letter stamps onto a large tag, and decorate by stitching on fabric embellishments of your choosing.

PROJECT 23

Bunting

Stamp flags on the patterned paper and cut out. Push the flags one by one through the sewing machine foot while slowly continuing to stitch.

What you'll need:
patterned paper,
flag stamps (Eline's baby flag set EC0108),
black inkpad,
scissors,
sewing machine

No. 249
DMC
BLANC

While embroidering I kept losing my thread, or more accurately the end of it. When I pulled on the end of a lovely new DMC skein, the whole thing immediately became all tangled up. And my curious cats didn't really help – quite the contrary! So in no time at all, my pretty DMC threads had turned into one big knot and all the wrappers with the colour numbers lay loose at the bottom of the bag. There must be a solution, I thought. So I made my own thread reels and it worked. Practical and tidy, with the numbers written on, the reels can be stored in a box or threaded onto a hoop to keep them all together.

PROJECT 24

DMC thread reels

Use a permanent marker to draw a line at the bottom of the circle punch, as an aid when punching semicircles. Punch out semicircles (or slightly less) from both sides of the labels. Punch out circles of patterned paper in various colours (to coordinate with the threads) and stick them at the top of the labels. Pierce through the holes. Using the Eline House label stamp, stamp the label image upside down (this way the number on the label stamp will be concealed under the threads) and stamp cross stitch borders at the base of the card labels. Write on the number of the DMC thread and wind the thread around the reel. Snip a notch into the label to secure the end of the thread.

What you'll need:
card labels,
2.5 cm (1 in) circle punch,
Eline's House patterned paper and stamps,
perforator,
DMC thread

Love you x x x

PROJECT 25

Pin cushion

Cut out a piece of patterned fabric measuring 13 x 20.5 cm (5 x 8¼ in) and a piece of linen measuring 13 x 5.5 cm (5 x 2¼ in) and add in seam allowances. Stitch the fabric and linen together along the 13 cm (5 in) edge; stitch a piece of lace along with a piece of ribbon over the seam to hide the join. Fold the fabric in half with right sides together and stitch around the edges, leaving a small gap for turning through and filling. After inserting the filling, blind-stitch the opening closed by hand.

Take a piece of patterned fabric featuring a rose and embroider the dark pink parts with small stitches by inserting the stitches very close together. Use this to cover the button (see Project 15). Attach the button along with the crocheted flower and a piece of ribbon in the middle of the front of the pin cushion. Draw the needle and thread through the cushion and attach a small button on the back to secure.

What you'll need:
'Vintage' patterned fabric,
linen fabric,
Eline's House ribbon,
fibrefill,
29 mm self-cover button,
crocheted flower,
sewing machine

The pretty embroidered fabric button is a lovely finishing touch.

AIR MAIL
2 cent

PROJECT 26

Fabric birds

Using the fabric bird pattern (see Patterns), cut the required pieces from your chosen fabrics, making sure you place the grain line on the straight grain of the fabric, parallel to the selvedge, and adding seam allowances. It's nice to vary the patterns and you can even use different patterns for the tail and the body by placing the design exactly over two patterns on the fabric.

Pin together the two sides of the bird with the right sides facing and stitch from the mark below the beak via the head and back to the tip of the tail. Now pin on the bird breast and tail piece and start stitching at the mark below the beak, first along one side and then along the other. Leave the end of the tail open. Trim the seams to 5 mm (1/4 in) and snip into the rounded sections. Turn the bird inside out via the tail: use the wrong end of a pencil to carefully push the bird's belly through the tail. This can be quite tricky when making a linen version, but as soon as a small part has been eased through the tail you can pull the rest through. Use a blunt stick to push all seams into shape and fill the bird fairly tightly via the tail. Do not insert any filling into the tail, and instead press this nice and flat. Cut off the end with pinking shears.

To make the wings, stitch two wing pieces together with right sides facing, leaving a small gap open so that you can turn them inside out. Press the seams flat. Alternatively, you can make the wings in the same way as my flower leaves (see Project 30), in which case the wings will contain wire and can be easily bent into shape. Use black thread to embroider the eyes by passing the needle through the head back and forwards a few times.
Sew on the wings with two buttons. Use a long needle to stitch right through the body, allowing you to attach them both at the same time. You can use a red or pink pencil to draw on the bird's rosy cheeks.

What you'll need:
fabric,
fibrefill,
buttons,
black thread,
(optional) double-sided adhesive plastic and thin wire

Bird in a box

Decorate the inside of the box with paper, stamps and lace. Cut holes in both sides and insert a branch. Sew the bird onto the branch with a few stitches.

What you'll need:
bird made from linen fabric and patterned wings,
pretty cardboard box,
small branch,
Eline's House patterned paper and stamps,
lace

AMSTERDAM CENTRAAL STATION
9 - 10N
30 - IV
1926
are red
Sugar

PROJECT 27

Bird on a string

Thread a needle with the red thread pull it through the bird from the centre of its back to its belly. Tie a knot under the belly. Attach beads, paper hearts and buttons to the strand underneath the bird's belly. Attach a paper heart to a short strand of thread and sew onto the beak.

What you'll need:
bird made from 'Meadow' fabric (see Project 26),
red DMC thread,
Eline's House patterned paper,
clay bead (see Project 6),
beads,
buttons

Home
Sweet
Home

PROJECT 28

Embroidered cushion

This cushion measures 40 x 40 cm (15⅝ x 15⅝ in). As I wasn't able to find all the thread colours under the same brand, I have used various different brands. The embroidery pattern (see Patterns) lists of the brands and colours I have used. As these threads are different thicknesses, for some threads I used a double strand and for the cotton even a triple strand. See the embroidery pattern key for details. Naturally you can purchase other brands, but make sure that the pink and red shades go well together, and the same for the three different greens and the two blues. If you prefer more vintage-style colours, replace the greens with beige shades and the blues with greyish blue.

Embroider the design in cross stitch. Then make an envelope back out of the linen fabric (see Project 21).

What you'll need:
coarse embroidery canvas
50 x 50 cm (20 x 20 in) with
nine holes per 5 cm (2 in),
wool and cotton in various
colours,
linen fabric,
sewing machine

A few branches from the woods and some coarse string make an original mobile.

PROJECT 29

Bird mobile

Sew the birds to the branches with a few large stitches. Use string to suspend the small branch from the large branch. Tie string to the large branch so that all the branches hang reasonably straight.

What you'll need:
a few fabric birds (see Project 26),
one large and one small branch,
string

PROJECT 30

Fabric flowers

Using the fabric flowers templates (see Patterns), cut two of each – one from patterned fabric and one from patterned paper. Stick the paper flower to the fabric version with double-sided adhesive plastic, but for the large flower, stick seven pieces of thin wire to the adhesive plastic first before sticking the fabric on top. Cut out the flowers along the pencil line. Cut along the line towards the centre as marked on the templates. Stick the two petals that appear on either side of this cut line together. To do this, carefully pull the fabric away from the back of one of the petals and cut off. Now place the sticky side over the adjacent petal, so that the flowers are no longer flat. Bend the petals of the large flower backwards. Roughly cut the leaves out of green fabric and stick two together with double-sided adhesive plastic, sandwiching a piece of thin wire in between. Leave the wire sticking out around 5 cm (2 in) at one side, so that you can use it to attach the leaf to the stem. Now cut out the leaves precisely.

Cover the buttons (see Project 15). Use a pair of pliers to make an eyelet at the end of the thick wire and attach a button to this. Now thread a crocheted flower, then the small flower and finally the large flower onto the wire and push everything to the top. Secure in place by wrapping double-sided adhesive plastic around the wire immediately beneath the flower head. Cut out a 2 cm (¾ in) diameter circle from double-sided adhesive plastic and make a cut up to the centre of the circle. Fold into a cone shape around the bottom of the flower head and the stem. Press to secure.

Use sticky tape to stick the wires of two or three leaves to the stem. Tear a strip of green fabric measuring around 3.5 x 35 cm (1⅜ x 13¾ in) and attach the end beneath the flower head. Twist the strip around the stem and allow the leaves to stick out in between. Fix securely to the bottom of the stem.

What you'll need:
'Meadow' patterned fabric,
Eline's House patterned paper,
29 mm self-cover button,
crocheted flowers,
double-sided adhesive plastic,
thin wire,
thick wire flower ties 40 cm (15⅝ in) long,
pair of pliers

PROJECT 31

Mini vases

With just a bit of patterned paper and some lace you can turn glass juice bottles into pretty vases. They're also great for displaying fresh flowers.

Use double-sided tape to stick pieces of patterned paper and ribbons to the bottles. Tie a piece of string around the neck of a bottle and thread clay beads onto the ends. Tie a ribbon around the neck of another bottle and stick a clay wax seal onto this.

What you'll need:
empty bottles,
Eline's House patterned paper and ribbon,
clay shapes (see Project 6),
double-sided tape,
string

Home sweet home

PROJECT 32

Key fobs cushions

Cut a piece of fabric measuring 7 x 14 cm (2¾ x 5½ in) and add in seam allowances. Fold in half with right sides facing. Fold a piece of ribbon in half and sandwich in between the folded fabric with the loop facing downward. Stitch around the edges, but leave a small gap for turning inside out. Insert the filling and stitch up the gap by hand. Decorate the cushion with embellishments and hang on a key ring.

What you'll need:
Eline's House fabric,
29 mm embroidered button (see Project 17),
ribbon (Ribbonstore),
crocheted flowers,
small stamped piece of linen fabric,
button,
fibrefill,
key rings

PROJECT 33

Little house

Trace the four little house pattern templates (see Patterns) onto fabric and add in seam allowances. Stitch seam A and press flat. Then stitch seams B for the roof of the house and press the seams flat. Lay down the front of the house with the right side facing up. Pin a piece of lace to the bottom of the house. Fold a piece of ribbon in half and position with the loop facing downward and the ends at the top over the apex of the roof. Now place the back of the house on top of this, with the right side facing down. Stitch around the edges, but leave a small gap for turning inside out and filling. Snip notches into the seam in all corners. Turn the house inside out and lightly fill with fibrefill. Stitch up the gap by hand. Sew the buttons onto the house and stitch the border along the roof. Attach the key ring to the ribbon loop.

What you'll need:
'Roses' patterned fabric,
23 mm fabric-covered button
(see Project 15),
fibrefill,
ribbon (Ribbonstore),
Eline's House lace and buttons,
key ring

You can make the prettiest files for your cards, photos or scrapbook items yourself.

PROJECT 34

Marianne's files

The size of the decorated file is determined by the size of the plastic folders that you have sourced to hold your cards, photos or scrapbook items. (You could even make a file for business cards.) Cut out the cardboard 5 mm (1/4 in) larger all around than your plastic folder. Cut out two pieces of patterned fabric that is 3 mm (1 1/8 in) larger all around than the cardboard.

Start by covering the outside of the file. Rub the cardboard with book binding glue and press firmly onto the patterned paper. Instead of a whole sheet you can also use two sheets, thus creating a wide range of patterns. Fold the flaps inwards and fold them open again; cut off the corners 5 mm (1/4 in) from the point of the cardboard. This can easily be done using a protractor and set square. Then fold the top and bottom flaps inwards and stick down. Fold and then stick down the side flaps. If you want to attach a ribbon, do this now, and cut the ribbon a little larger than the height of the file so that you can fold it over the back. Use a pencil and ruler to draw a line where the ribbon needs to go, and trace this line with book binding glue using a paintbrush. Stick down the ribbon on the back of the covers.

Now cut the paper for the inside of the covers. Re-measure the cardboard and deduct 5 mm (1/4 in) from the length and the width. If you use these measurements when cutting the paper it will fit perfectly on the inside. Rub the inside of the covers with book binding glue and stick the paper down.

Place the plastic folder inside the cardboard and mark out the holes with pencil. Pierce or punch through the holes (in both cardboard parts). Push the metal rings through the covers and the folde,r and click shut. Decorate the rings with ribbons and/or crocheted flowers and decorate the front of the file with cut-out paper birds (see Patterns). You can decorate the birds with backstitch using three strands of DMC thread, and sew buttons onto the wings. Attach the birds to the file using foam tape.

What you'll need:

- stiff cardboard (grey board),
- Eline's House patterned paper and ribbon,
- book binding glue,
- plastic folders,
- protractor and set square
- metal rings (with a fastener),
- crocheted flowers,
- DMC thread,
- hole punch,
- buttons,
- various ribbons,
- foam tape

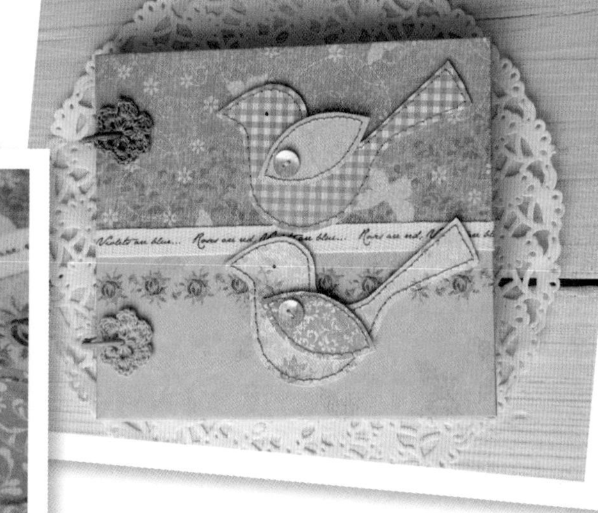

Roses are red,
Violets are blue,
Sugar is sweet,
and so are you.

PROJECT 35

Little white tree

Search for a few branches in pretty shapes and paint them white (choose a primer that has good covering power). Stick a piece of double-sided tape to the back of the vase and wrap the flower garland around the vase. Sew the birds to the branches with a few large stitches. Place the branches in the vase and hang on the hearts.

What you'll need:
lots of little fabric hearts (see Project 36),
a few little fabric birds (see Project 26),
branches,
white primer,
vase,
crocheted flower garland,
double-sided tape

Crocheted flower garland

Tear strips of fabric approx. 3 cm (1⅛ in) wide and tie together loosely. Sew crocheted flowers, leaves and butterflies here and there onto the strips.

What you'll need:
'Meadow' patterned fabric,
crocheted designs (see Project 46),
crochet hook 2.5–3 mm

I wrapped the crocheted flower garland around a simple vase as a decoration.

2 cent

PROJECT 36

Antoinette's little hearts

Cut out little hearts (see Patterns) from scraps of fabric and felt, and add in a seam allowance of 5 mm (1/4 in). Copy the bird A, rose B and butterfly C embroidery outlines (see Patterns) onto paper and roughly cut out. Stick the paper to the fabric hearts with tape and carefully embroider the illustration with a backstitch or chain stitch through the paper and the fabric. Once you've finished embroidering, carefully cut the paper off.

To make the felt and fabric flower, cut the flower appliqué D (see Patterns) from scraps of fabric and felt. Sew the flower to the heart with embroidery stitches using DMC threads. Sew a button in the centre of the flower.

Cut a piece of ribbon or trim measuring approx. 10 cm (4 in) and fold double. Pin the back of the heart, a layer of fibrefill cut to the exact size of the little heart template, the ribbon and the front of the heart together. Make sure that the front and back match or go well together. Stitch the hearts together with a blanket stitch, backstitch or chain stitch.

What you'll need:
scraps of patterned fabric, felt and linen fabric,
DMC thread,
Eline's House buttons,
fibrefill,
pieces of trim,
crocheted flower and butterfly (see Project 46),
picot lace flowers (see Project 47)

Home sweet home

PROJECT 37

Gepke's bird box

Paint the bird box white with acrylic paint (masonry paint is fine). Make a template of the front of the box. Cut out the template and check that it fits exactly onto the box. Press the outline of the heart into the paper template with your fingers and cut this out. Check again that everything is in the right place. Use the paper template to cut a front and back out of the linen fabric, and cut the heart shape out of the front. Print stamps onto the linen fabric front and back. Stick down the ribbons with double-sided tape. Rub the back of the box with Chemage and stick the linen on. Stick the linen on the front in the same way. For the sides, cut out two pieces of fabric to fit; rub the box with Chemage and stick the fabric on.

For the roof, cut out a piece of fabric and a strip of fibrefill each measuring 31 x 12 cm ($12\frac{3}{8}$ x $4\frac{3}{4}$ in), and stitch together with a large zigzag stitch. Apply a line of textile adhesive to the roof and stick on the fabric/fibrefill strip. Carefully secure the edges with pegs so that it can dry in place. Use textile adhesive to stick a 5 mm ($\frac{1}{4}$ in) lace border along the front and back edge to conceal the zigzag stitch. Decorate the roof as in the photograph or as you like.

Make a little bird as described (see Project 26) and stick or sew it on in front of the box.

What you'll need:
wooden bird box with heart-shaped window (Your Zoap),
white acrylic paint,
'Roses' patterned fabric,
linen fabric,
fibrefill,
Eline's House ribbons and buttons,
DMC thread,
Eline's House stamps,
black inkpad,
Chemage (découpage adhesive),
textile adhesive,
double-sided tape

PROJECT 38

Bags

Blue bag

Cut the bag pieces to size:
Front and back: 32 x 24 cm ($12\frac{1}{2}$ x $9\frac{1}{2}$ in) and add in all seam allowances – cut two pieces of patterned fabric, two pieces of linen fabric and two pieces of fibrefill
Connecting strip: 13 x 80 cm (5 x $31\frac{3}{8}$ in) – cut two pieces of linen fabric and one piece of fibrefill
For the handles: cut two pieces of linen fabric measuring 35 x 6 cm (14 x $2\frac{3}{8}$ in) or as long as desired

Stitch a piece of ribbon from the top to the bottom along one side of the front piece of the patterned fabric. Hand-stitch the crocheted doily onto this. Sew a crocheted flower to this with a button, with a small piece of ribbon sticking out. Now stitch one of the connecting linen fabric strips to the patterned fabric front and back to complete the outer bag.

Zigzag the fibrefill pieces to the linen pieces and stitch these parts together to create an inner bag. Leave a 15 cm ($5\frac{6}{8}$ in) section open at the bottom so that you can turn the bag inside out. Fold the strips for the handles double, stitch the long sides together and turn the strips inside out. Fold the strips so that the seam is at the centre of the back and press flat. Stitch a strip of lace over the handles. Stitch the handles, with right sides facing, to the outer bag 8 cm ($3\frac{1}{8}$ in) from the side. Position the inner bag and the outer bag with the right sides facing. Stitch the top edges together, watching out for the handles. Turn the bag inside out through the opening on the inside. Stitch the opening shut by hand. Cut two pieces of ribbon measuring 40 cm (16 in) and sew this to the top corners of the bag with a button. Sew on a crocheted flower with a button. Tie the ribbon together to create a fold.

What you'll need:
'Vintage' patterned fabric,
linen fabric,
fibrefill,
crocheted flowers,
crocheted doily,
Eline's House ribbon and buttons,
sewing machine

Linen key cord

Cut a strip measuring 110 x 6 cm ($43\frac{1}{8}$ x $2\frac{3}{8}$ in) adding a 1 cm ($\frac{3}{8}$ in) seam allowance. Work a zigzag stitch around the edges of the strip. Stitch the alphabet trim 2 cm ($\frac{3}{4}$ in) down from one of the long edges. Fold the strip in half lengthways with right sides facing, push through the D ring and stitch the short side to create a circle. Fold the fabric double and turn in the hem on both sides. Stitch through the edges. Attach the D ring at 4.5 cm ($1\frac{3}{4}$ in). Make two leaves out of ribbon and sew the flower on top of the leaves. Sew the whole thing to the key cord. Sew a button onto the flower. Attach the key fob to the D ring.

What you'll need:
linen fabric,
3 cm ($1\frac{1}{8}$ in) wide D ring,
detachable key fob,
alphabet trim,
crocheted five-petal flower,
Eline's House ribbon and buttons

2 cent
1 cent
ABCDEFGHIJKLMNOPQRSTUVWXYZ

Linen bag

Using the linen bag pattern (see Patterns), cut two pieces (front and back) from linen fabric and two pieces (lining) from the patterned fabric allowing for a 1 cm (3/8 in) seam allowance. Also cut a linen fabric and patterned fabric connecting strip measuring 10 x 114 cm (4 x 44 5/8 in) without a seam. Cut a strip measuring 10 x 88 cm (4 x 34½ in) for the handles and 7 x 9 cm (2¾ x 3½ in) for the loop for the key fob. Finish the pieces with a zigzag stitch. For the bag front embellishments, cut the following from the 'Vintage' fabric: a 23 x 23cm (9 x 9 in) piece featuring the embroidered red rose, a circle with the lace border, two postage stamps. Reinforce these embellishment pieces with interfacing if desired and pin, along with the trims, in an attractive arrangement on one of the linen pieces to make the bag front. Use a running stitch and the pink DMC thread to sew the rose square to the front, sew on the postage stamps with a smaller stitch, and embroider over a number of the cross stitches in the rose. Finally, stitch on the trims and the lace-bordered circle.

To assemble the bag, pin the 10 x 114 cm (4 x 44 5/8 in) linen connecting strip to the bag front and stitch. Repeat for the back. Topstitch along the seams. Hem the bag at the top.

Fold the handle strip in half lengthways and turn in the hem. Stitch along either side. Stitch a beige/pink trim to the middle of the hemmed strip. Sew a loop for the key fob in the same way. Cut the handles into two equal lengths, and attach the D ring to the loop. Pin the handles with the right side facing on the bag front. Also pin the D ring to the edge of the bag.

Turn the lining so that the right side is on the inside. Slide the lining over the outside of the bag so that both fit together; stitch around the edge, but leave a gap of about 12 cm (4¾ in) for turning through.

Turn the bag the right way out; fold in the hems of the gap, and stitch closed. Topstitch along the edge. Use ribbon loops to attach the crocheted heart and fabric heart to the detachable key fob to finish.

What you'll need:
'Vintage' patterned fabric,
linen fabric,
interfacing,
Eline's House ribbon,
alphabet trim (Ribbonstore) pink thread,
3 cm (1 1/8 in) wide D ring,
DMC thread 603,
crocheted flower and heart (see Project 46),
patterned fabric heart (see Project 36),
detachable key fob

ELINE

Coat hook bag

Using the coat hook bag pattern (see Patterns), cut two pieces (front and back) from the patterned fabric, making sure that the edge of the rose pattern is about a third from the top. Also cut two pieces for the lining from the embroidered rose section. Cut two connecting strips measuring 88 x 7.5 cm (34½ x 3 in) and a strip measuring 70 x 9 cm (27½ x 3½ in) for the handles. Finish the sections with a zigzag stitch.

Embroider your name onto the Aida with two strands of DMC thread 321. Embroider the box around the name. Count five threads around the embroidery and cut out the Aida. Use DMC thread 581 to sew the embroidered patch to the front of the bag. Fray the edges and sew on the two buttons.

To assemble the bag, fold a piece of ribbon measuring 8 cm (3⅛ in) in half and pin it to the side of the bag (see photo). Pin the 88 x 7.5 cm (34½ x 3 in) connecting strip to the front of the bag and stitch. Repeat for the back. Topstitch along the seams. Assemble the lining in the same way as the outside of the bag.

For the handle, fold the strip in half lengthways and turn in the hem. Stitch along either side. Cut off 20 cm (8 in) for the short handle. Pin the handles with the right side facing on the bag front. Turn the lining so that the right side is on the inside. Slide the lining over the ouside of the bag so that both fit together. Stitch around the edge, but leave a gap of about 12 cm (4¾ in) for turning through.

Turn the bag out the right way; fold the seams inwards to hem the gap, and stitch closed. Topstitch along the edge. The bag is closed by pushing the large loop through the small loop. To finish, sew on the crocheted embellishments.

What you'll need:
'Meadow' patterned fabric,
white 14-count Aida,
DMC threads 321 and 581,
Eline's House buttons,
crocheted flowers and leaves,
piece of ribbon,
sewing machine

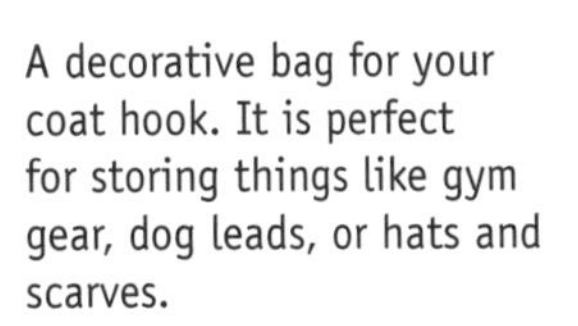

A decorative bag for your coat hook. It is perfect for storing things like gym gear, dog leads, or hats and scarves.

het is
Jouw
verjaardag
2 cent
5 cent
1 cent

PROJECT 39

Linen pouch with felt flower

Cut out two pieces of linen measuring 16 x 12 cm (6¼ x 4¾ in), which includes a 1 cm (⅜ in) seam allowance, and a piece of green fabric with text measuring 12 x 7.5 cm (4¾ x 3 in). Cut a 6 cm (2⅜ in) diameter circle out of pink felt, a smaller 3 cm (1⅛ in) diameter circle out of light pink felt, the brooch appliqué flower centre (see Patterns) out of ecru and four leaves out of khaki-coloured felt. Finish the linen with a zigzag stitch around the edge and mark the centre with a chalk line.

Sew the green rectangle with a blanket stitch in the centre of one of the pieces of linen fabric. Place the felt circles and the flower on top of each other according to the photo and sew on the flower with a backstitch and the small circle with a chain stitch. Sew the circle to the pouch with a double row of running stitches. Sew a button in the centre of the felt flower. Embroider the leaves on with a chain stitch using a green thread.

Measure the zip on the top, place the two linen pieces with right sides facing and stitch the seams at the top up to the zip opening. Put in the zip using a sewing machine. Backstitch by hand with two strands of DMC thread along the zip opening. Machine stitch along the three sides of the pouch. Cut the corners on the bias and turn the pouch inside out. Decorate the zip pull with a small piece of ribbon.

What you'll need:
piece of linen fabric and
'Meadow' patterned fabric,
12 cm (4¾ in) white or natural
coloured zip,
felt in various colours,
DMC thread,
piece of ribbon,
Eline's House buttons,
sewing machine

< Postcard rack with examples of Eline's House patterned paper.

tains, with light and song,
which tell of the violet's birth,
eaves opening as I pass.
thousands have burst from the forest flowers
wreathes on Italian plains;
ruin on the tomb!
ch has hung all his tassels forth,
s o'er the pastures free,
s bright, where my step has been,
d out each voice of the deep blue sky,
oves of the soft Hesperian clime,
e fir branch into verdure breaks,
e sweeping on to the silvery main,
flinging spray o'er the forest boughs
th resounds with the joy of waves

PROJECT 40

Brooches

If desired, reinforce one of the circles with interfacing as the base for the brooch. Cut circles and flowers (see Patterns) out of the patterned fabrics. Use a blanket stitch or chain stitch to attach the small circle to the large circle, and use a different colour to attach the flower(s) to the circle with a few chain stitches. Leave the ends of the petals loose. Sew a button at the centre of the flower if desired. Sew the brooch pin onto the back.

What you'll need:
pieces of 'Meadow' and 'Vintage' patterned fabric,
interfacing,
DMC thread in various colours,
Eline's House buttons,
brooch pins

280
No. Butterfly
Specimen

Flowers from the garden

I have always loved gardening ever since I was a little girl. Because I only have a balcony in the city, a few years ago I set out to look for an allotment. Since then I have been the proud owner of a little green paradise just a 15 minute drive from my house. I don't grow vegetables, but I have heaps of flowers, a pond and a patch of grass with daisies. The pink Hortensia and deep-purple Clematis are currently in full bloom, and I often bring home a bunch to display in a vase. Flowers from my own garden is my way of bringing a bit of nature to the city.

This romantic bunting made of patches of cloth and folded lace paper makes a birthday or wedding even more festive.

PROJECT 41

Frences' festive bunting

For the lace flags, fold a large piece of lace paper into a point by folding the two sides diagonally across one another and then turning back the top. The top must be 18 cm (7 in) wide and the sides 24 cm (9½ in) long. For the fabric flags, cut out pieces of patterned fabric and linen measuring 10 x 17 cm (4 x 6¾ in).

Apply adhesive spray to the lace paper flags and a small amount of textile adhesive to the surface where there are no holes. Fold the top part around the string and stick down. For the fabric flags, first apply a thin layer of textile adhesive to one side of the lace paper doily and stick this side to the fabric, then apply a layer to the other side, fold this around the string and stick to the fabric at the back.

You can decorate the paper and fabric flags with any materials you like.

What you'll need:
sheets of lace paper,
'Vintage' patterned fabric,
linen fabric,
string,
adhesive spray,
textile adhesive,
embellishments of your choosing

PETITE
20 old-fashioned buttons
produced by: www.mariannedesign.nl
20
Piano

PROJECT 42

Butterfly garland

Print butterfly stamps onto the front or back of patterned paper and cut them out. Using a sewing machine, push the butterflies one by one through the foot. Stitch through them horizontally and allow the thread to run between the butterflies.

What you'll need:
Eline's House patterned paper and butterfly stamps,
black inkpad,
sewing machine

Love you x x x

PROJECT 43

Lampshade

Copy the small rose embroidery pattern A (see Patterns) three times and cut out with a border of about 1 cm (3/8 in). Fold out the lampshade according to the instructions. Use the adhesive tape to attach the roses to the lampshade and pierce the holes with the hole punch. Be careful! The rice paper is fragile! Embroider the rose designs in backstitch using the full thickness (i.e. six strands) of the DMC thread and a backstitch. Stick the fastening thread to the inside of the lampshade with adhesive tape and use a needle with a blunt tip.

What you'll need:
rice paper globe lampshade (Ikea),
very fine hole punch,
non-permanent adhesive tape,
DMC thread

Antoinette had a tough job embroidering this rice paper lampshade. A challenge for those with plenty of patience and excellent hand-eye coordination.

The pattern for this clutch purse is a circle simply folded up and secured. It is perfect for storing small items in your bag, paper tissues for instance.

PROJECT 44

Clutch purse

Cut two 25 cm (10 in) diameter circles out of the fabric, adding a 1 cm ($\frac{3}{8}$ in) seam allowance all around. Stitch a ribbon across the centre of the circle from 2 cm ($\frac{3}{4}$ in) from the top to 8 cm ($3\frac{1}{8}$ in) from the bottom. Pin the ends of the ribbon down in the middle so that they do not get caught in between the seam. Place the circles with the right sides facing and stitch all around the edge, leaving a gap of 6 cm ($2\frac{3}{8}$ in) gap for turning inside out. Make small snips in the seam up to the stitching line and turn the bag inside out. Hem the opening shut and topstitch around the border. Fold the lower edge 8 cm ($3\frac{1}{8}$ in) towards the centre and the side flaps 5.5 cm ($2\frac{1}{4}$ in) towards the centre. Fasten down the flaps with a mother-of-pearl button. Make a butterfly out of two colours of felt and DMC thread (see Patterns). Sew the butterfly to the flap of the bag.

What you'll need:
'Meadow' patterned fabric,
Eline's House ribbon,
Eline's House buttons,
DMC thread,
felt,
sewing machine

603
644
3348
ROSES
1 cent
2 cent

Roses are red Violets are blue Sugar is sweet And so are You

PROJECT 45

Key cord

Cut a strip measuring 6 x 92 cm (2³/₈ x 36 in) with a 1 cm (³/₈ in) seam allowance. Sew a zigzag stitch around the edges of the strip. Place the strip with the right sides facing, push the D ring through the fabric and stitch the short side to create a circle. Fold the fabric double and turn the hem in on both sides. Use a decorative stitch to stitch through both sides of the key cord. Sew on a piece of trim with the text 'Roses are red, Violets are blue' and sew a small crocheted flower with a few small pieces of ribbon to the key cord. Sew the butterfly to the key fob and tie on a ribbon.

What you'll need:
'Vintage' patterned fabric,
3 cm (1¹/₈ in) wide D ring,
detachable key fob,
Eline's House ribbon,
crocheted geranium flower
and blue/white butterfly
(see Project 46),
white sewing thread,
sewing machine

Crochet patterns

Crocheted flowers are used often throughout this book. It is nice to crochet them yourself, but for those who prefer not to you can buy them ready-made. The Crochet Flowers by Marianne Design are very pretty, delicate flowers in various colours and sizes. Those who want to make their own embellishments can follow these instructions:

Marianne's flowers

5 chains, close to a ring with a slip stitch. Row 1: 7 chains and *1 double treble crochet in the ring, 3 chains*, repeat this 7 times and close with a slip stitch in the 4th chain in this row. Row 2: then in the arc: 1 double crochet, 1 treble crochet, 3 double treble crochets, 1 treble crochet and 1 double crochet, repeat this 7 times and fasten off with a slip stitch.

Gerbera

Crochet 6 chains in pink, close with a slip stitch to a ring. Row 1: 1 times chains, 11 double crochets in the ring and close with a slip stitch. Row 2: with white *12 chains and 1 double crochet in the double crochet. *Repeat this 11 times and fasten off with a slip stitch.

Open five-petal flower

Colour 1: 5 chains, close to a ring with a slip stitch. Row 1: 3 chain, 1 treble crochet in the ring *2 chains, 2 treble crochets in the ring*, repeat this 4 times and end with a slip stitch in the 3rd chain of the row.

Row 2: change colour, 1 chain, *2 double crochets in the underlying double crochets, then crochet 4 treble crochets in the arc*. Repeat this 4 times and fasten off with a slip stitch.

Geranium

4 chains in green, close with a slip stitch. Row 1: 1 chain and 5 double crochets in the ring, finish with a slip stitch in the first chain. Row 2: change colour. Use a colour such as pink to crochet *4 chains and 3 double treble crochets in the underlying double crochet, finish the petal with 3 chains and a slip stitch in the same underlying double crochet*. Repeat this 4 times and fasten off with a double crochet.

Leaves

Crochet 9 chains. This is the vein of the leaf. Now crochet 1 times double crochet in the 2nd last chain. Followed by a half treble crochet, 2 treble crochets, double treble crochet, 2 treble crochets and half treble crochet. Crochet 3 double crochets in the last remaining chain. For the other side of the leaf, crochet into the same chains that have already been crocheted into, then a half treble crochet, 2 treble crochets, double treble crochet, 2 treble crochets, half treble crochet and fasten off with a slip stitch in the 1st double crochet. You can vary the curvature of the leaf by using more or fewer half treble crochets, treble crochets and double treble crochets.

Butterfly

Crochet 8 chains in blue, close with a slip stitch to a ring. Row 1: crochet 3 chains and 2 double treble crochets in the ring. Followed by *3 chains and 3 double treble crochets*, repeat another 6 times. Crochet another 3 chains with a slip stitch to the 3rd chain of the 1st row. Row 2: in the arcs crochet 1 double crochet, 1 treble crochet, 3 double treble crochets, 1 treble crochet and 1 double crochet, repeat this 7 times. You will be left with a flower that is not completely flat. Fold the flower double. Body of the butterfly: crochet 7 chains. Now crochet 1 double crochet in the second last chain. Pull through the left of the crocheted double crochet and crochet a double crochet, repeat this 12 times. Make a slip stitch at the point where you started to crochet double crochets and make another 6 chains. Fasten off. The body will be twice as thick as with normal chains. Slide the body over the butterfly and push into shape.

Little heart

Crochet a chain of 6 chain stitches and close with a slip stitch. Row 1: crochet 1 chain and 9 double crochets in the ring, close with a slip stitch. Row 2: crochet 1 chain and 1 double crochet. Now crochet in the next double crochet of the ring 2 treble crochets, 2 double treble crochets and 2 treble crochets. This is the curve of the heart. Crochet 2 half treble crochets in the next double crochets. In the next double crochet 1 half treble crochet, 2 treble crochets and 1 half treble crochet; this is the point of the heart. Now crochet, in this order, 2 half treble crochets in the next double crochets and 2 treble crochets, 2 double treble crochets, 2 treble crochets in 1 double crochet, then close the row with a slip stitch. Row 3: crochet a row of double crochets in a different colour. Increase (2 double crochets in 1 double crochet) in the curve and in the point of the heart. Row 4: crochet a braid stitch in the base colour as a finishing touch. Pull the loop of the crochet hook through the back right of the double crochet and crochet 1 double crochet, not clockwise, but anticlockwise. Fasten off.

Sew the flowers to a piece of lace to make a pretty shelf edging.

PROJECT 47

Little flowers made from picot lace

Cut a piece of lace measuring around 15 cm (5⅝ in). Select a DMC thread in a nice colour. Push the crochet hook through the second hole in the lace and pull up one loop. Now push through each hole and pull up one loop, so that there are several loops on the crochet hook. Stop at the second last hole and then fasten off by pulling the DMC thread strand through all loops. Fasten off and sew the start and end of the lace together with white thread to make a rosette.

What you'll need:

Eline's House picot lace ribbon,

DMC thread,

2.5–3 mm crochet hook,

white sewing thread

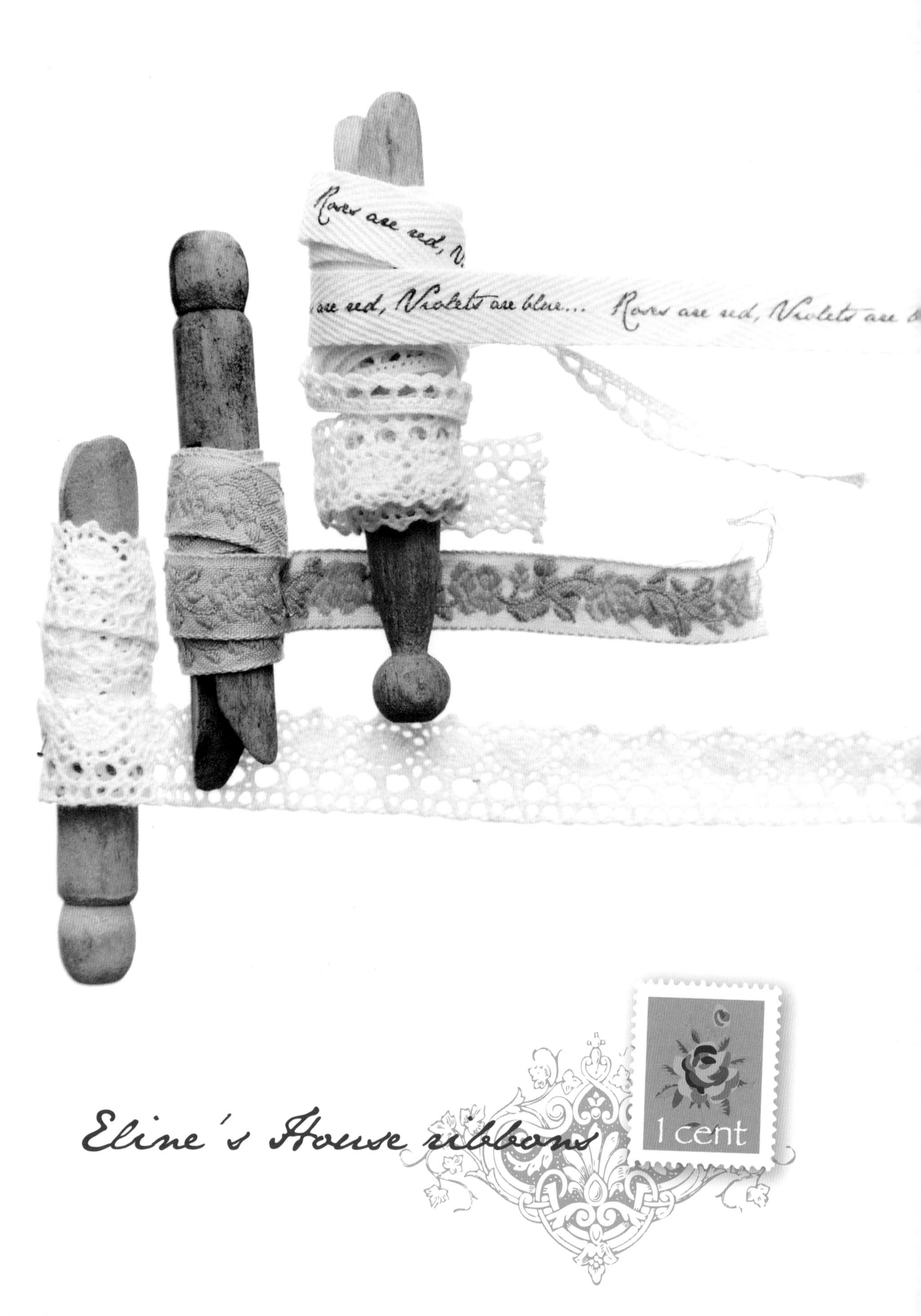

Eline's House ribbons

Embroidery stitches

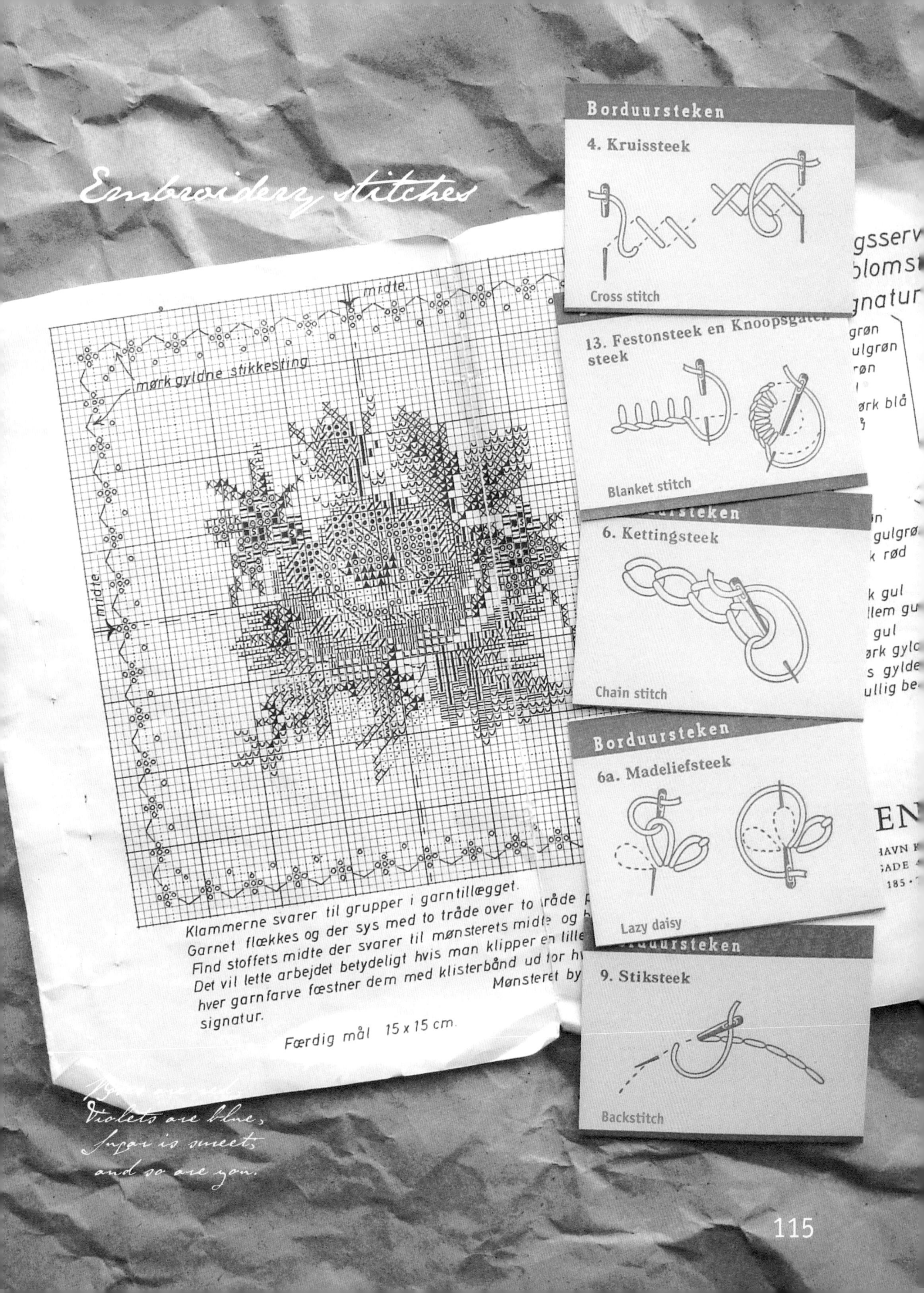

Roses are red,
Violets are blue,
Sugar is sweet,
and so are you.

Patterns

DMC colours

Colour	Name	DMC
	White	BLANC
	Winter white	3865
	Light green grey	644
	Dark antique silver	3032
	Igloo blue	3841
	Light blue	813
	Lettuce heart green	3348
	Grasshopper green	581
	Marshmallow rose	151
	Sweet pink	603
	Fuchsia	601
	Red	321
	Mouse grey	168
	Pewter grey	169
	Black	310

cross stitch charts

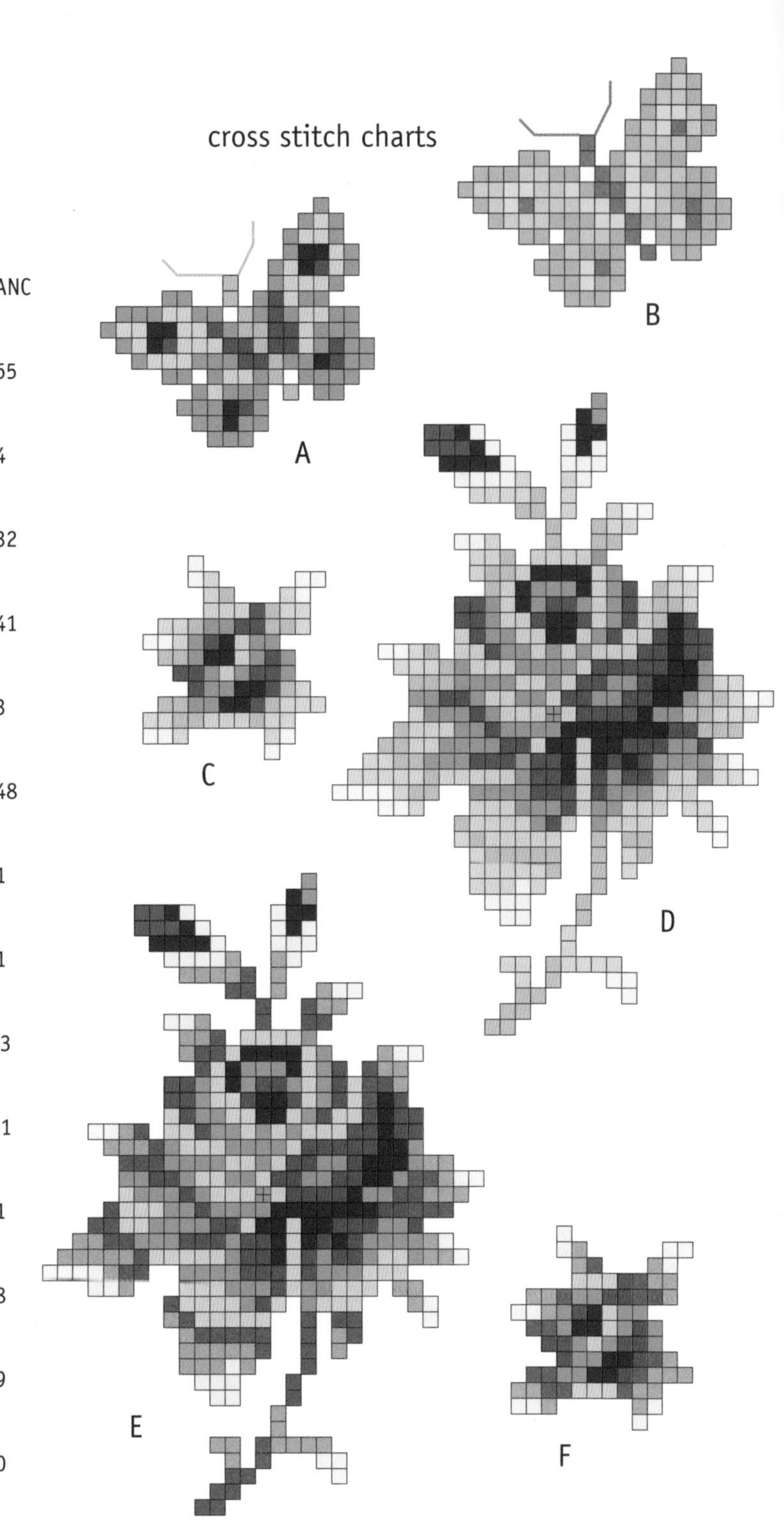

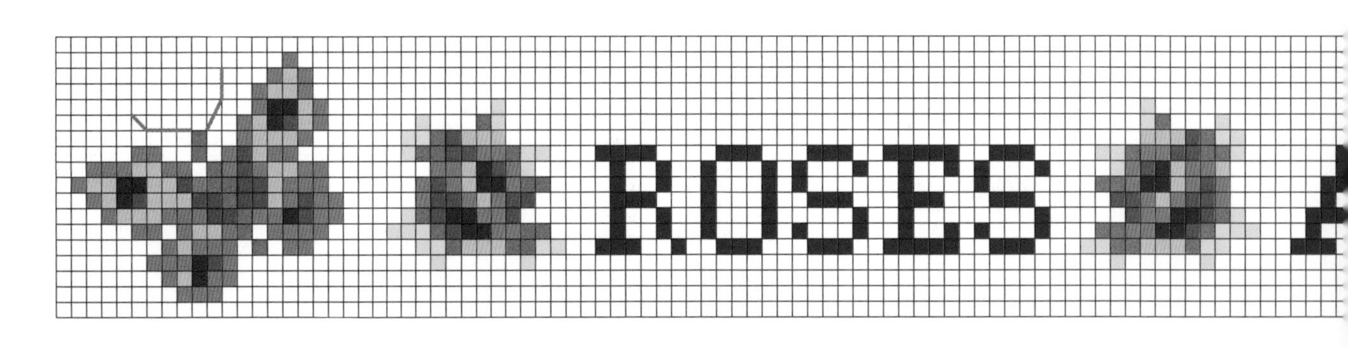

G

I

H

J

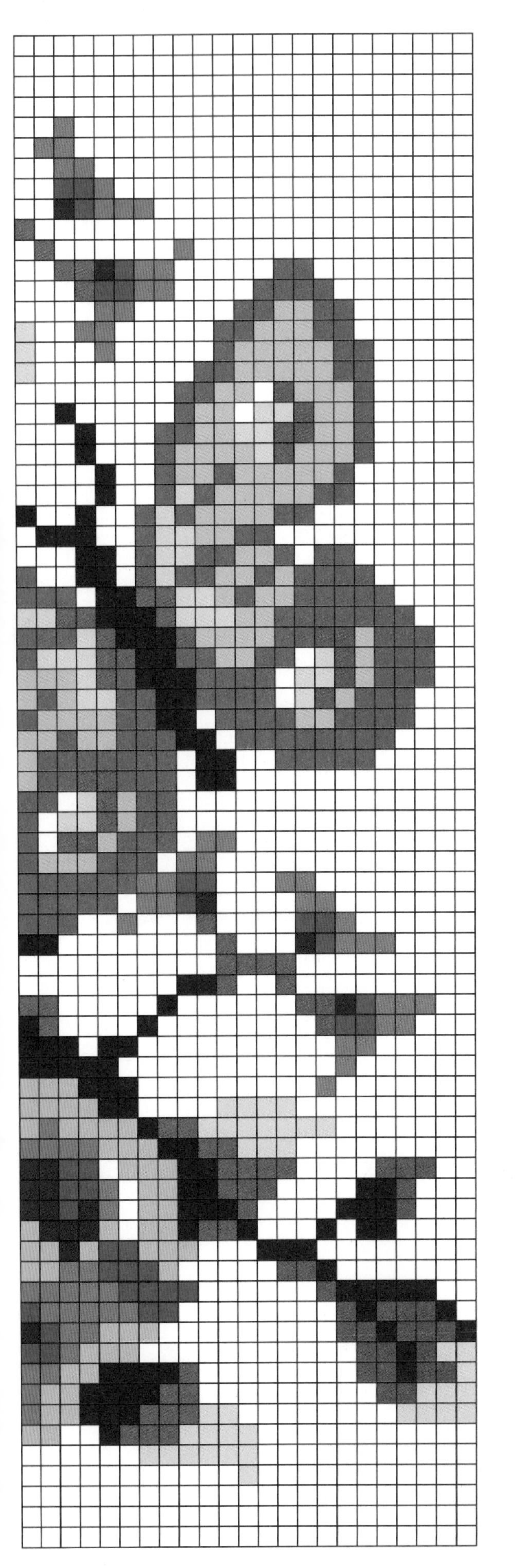

Embroidered cushion

embroidery patterns

Online linie 50 Prima colour 0001 (double strand) base, you will need two balls of yarn

Online linie 152 Paloma colour 0014 (double strand)

Bravo Baby Schachenmayr nomotta colour 00136 (double strand)

Online linie 165 Sandy colour 36 cotton (triple strand)

Bravo Baby Schachenmayr nomotta colour 00130 (double strand)

Planet colour 3980 (single strand)

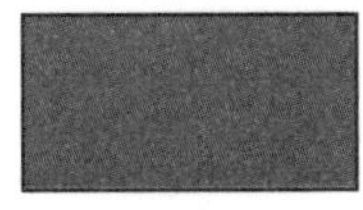

Planet colour 3983 (single strand)

Larra Markoma colour 7352 cotton (triple strand)

Planet colour 3953 (single strand)

Bravo Schachenmayr nomotta colour 08259 (double strand)

Little hearts

embroidery outlines

Brooch

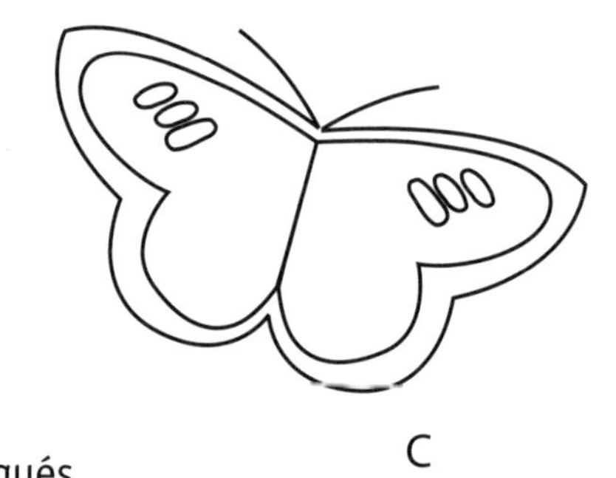

appliqués

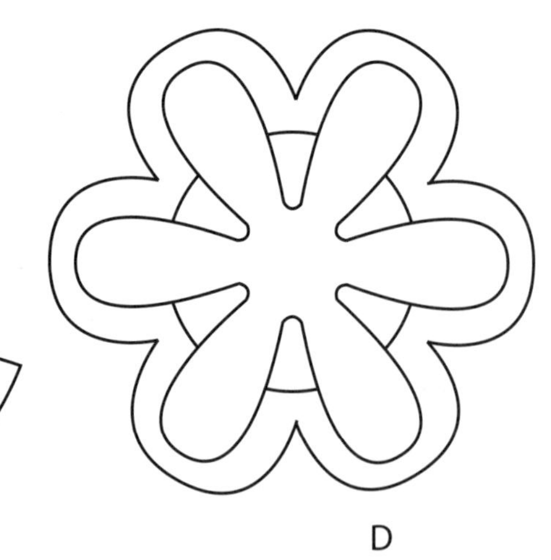

Roses

embroidery patterns

Birds

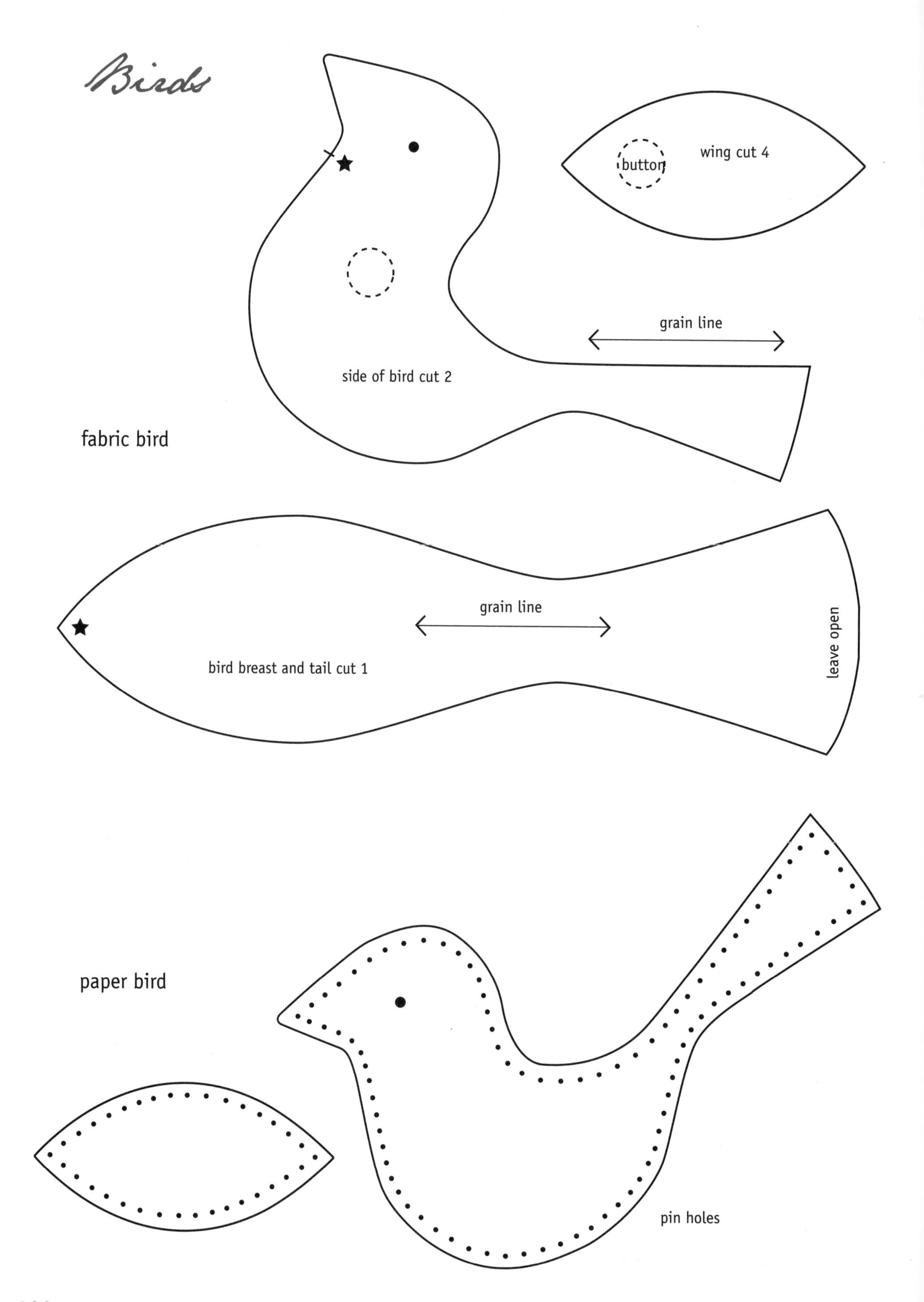

button
wing cut 4
grain line
side of bird cut 2
fabric bird
grain line
bird breast and tail cut 1
leave open
paper bird
pin holes

Little House

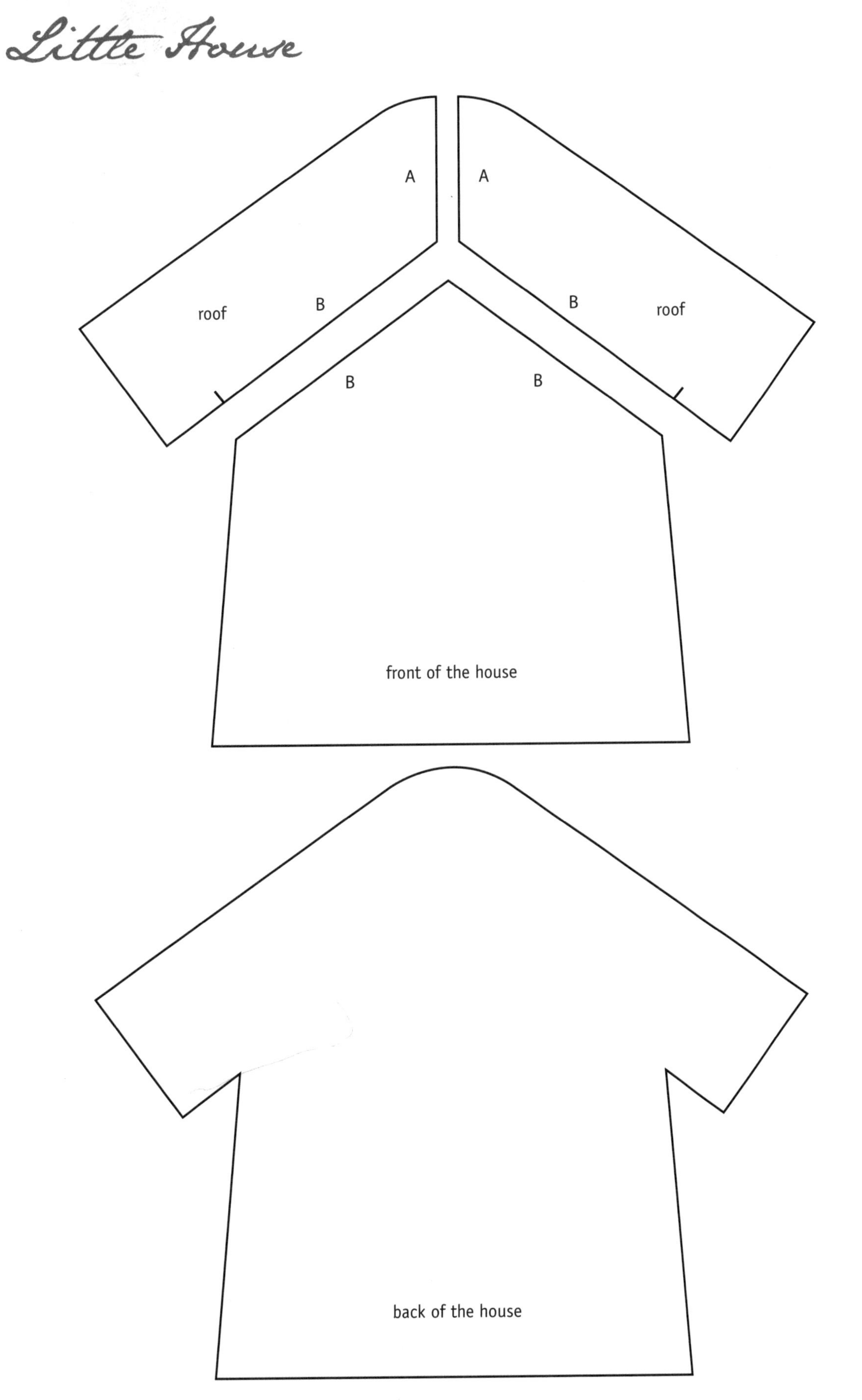

Fabric flowers

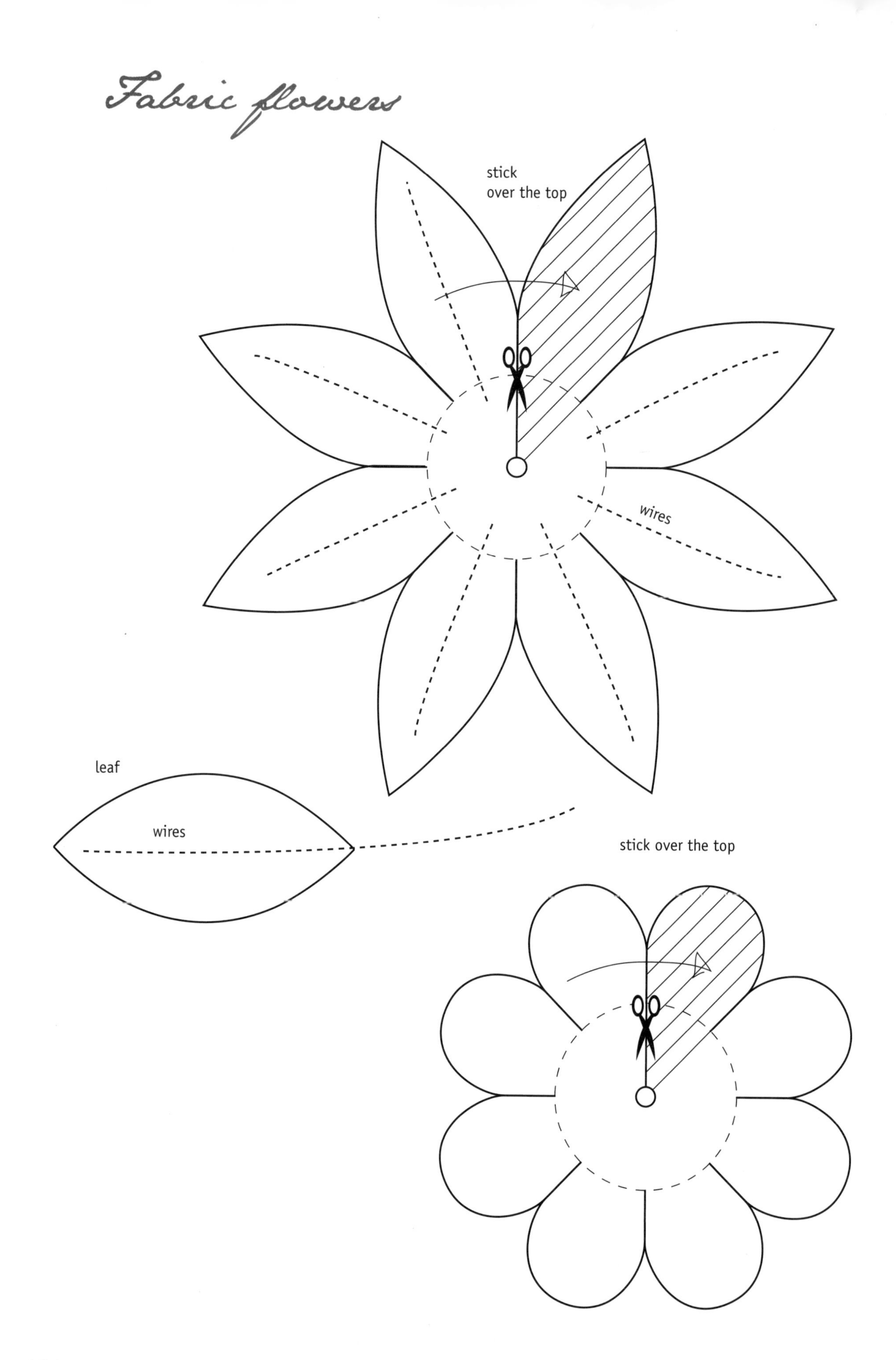

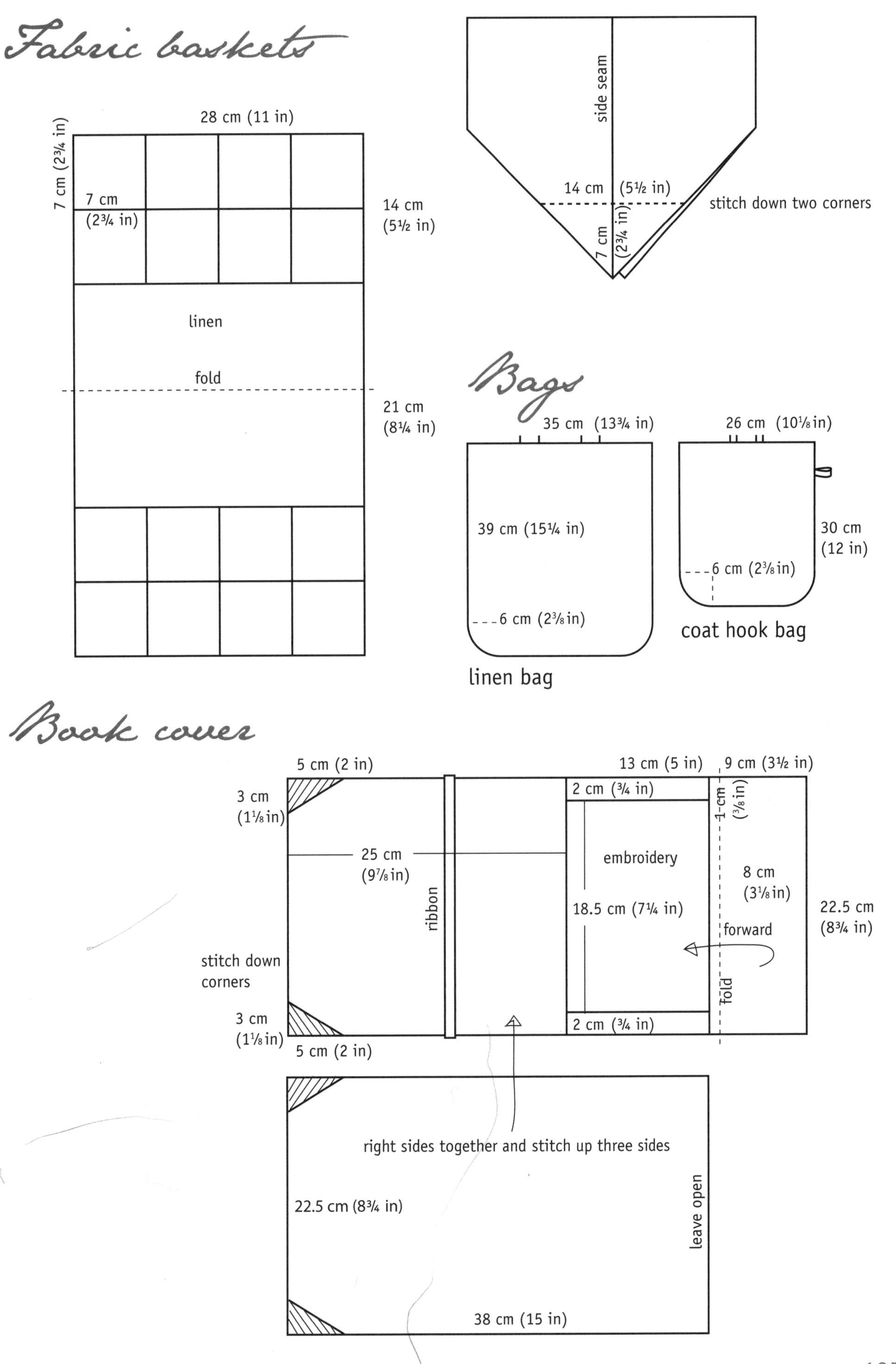
Fabric baskets
28 cm (11 in)
7 cm (2¾ in)
7 cm
(2¾ in)
14 cm
(5½ in)
linen
fold
21 cm
(8¼ in)
side seam
14 cm (5½ in)
stitch down two corners
7 cm
(2¾ in)
Bags
35 cm (13¾ in)
39 cm (15¼ in)
6 cm (2⅜ in)
linen bag
26 cm (10⅛ in)
30 cm
(12 in)
6 cm (2⅜ in)
coat hook bag
Book cover
5 cm (2 in)
3 cm
(1⅛ in)
25 cm
(9⅞ in)
ribbon
stitch down
corners
3 cm
(1⅛ in)
5 cm (2 in)
13 cm (5 in)
9 cm (3½ in)
2 cm (¾ in)
1 cm
(⅜ in)
embroidery
8 cm
(3⅛ in)
18.5 cm (7¼ in)
forward
fold
2 cm (¾ in)
22.5 cm
(8¾ in)
right sides together and stitch up three sides
22.5 cm (8¾ in)
leave open
38 cm (15 in)

Cushion covers

stencils

Enlarge these two designs by 140% using a photocopier.
Stick a plastic sheet to the copy with adhesive tape and cut out the black parts.

transfer

Scan this postage stamp, print it (in reverse) onto transfer paper and iron onto white cotton.

With thanks to...

With thanks to photographer Joost de Wolf (www.jdwfotografie.nl), who took most of the photographs in this book. He captured all of my ideas perfectly, even when this meant literally having to bend over backwards.

Thanks also to photographer Hans Guldemond (www.hansguldemond.nl) for composing and taking the portrait photo on the back cover.

Index